P9-DZY-510

STEP-BY-STEP

Chinese and Wok Cooking

STEP-BY-STEP

Chinese and Wok Cooking

Shirley Gill

Photographs by Amanda Heywood

SMITHMARK

© Anness Publishing Limited 1996

All rights reserved. No part of this publication may be
reproduced, stored in a retrieval system, or transmitted in
any way or by any means, electronic, mechanical,
photocopying, recording or otherwise, without the prior
permission of the copyright holder.

This edition published in 1996 by
SMITHMARK Publishers a division of U.S. Media Holdings Inc.
16 East 32nd Street
New York
NY 10016

SMITHMARK books are available for bulk purchase for sales
promotion and for premium use. For details write or call
the Manager of Special Sales, SMITHMARK Publishers Inc.
16 East 32nd Street, New York, NY, 10016; (212) 5326600

Produced by Anness Publishing Limited
1 Boundary Row
London SE1 8HP

Printed and bound in Hong Kong

10 9 8 7 6 5 4 3 2 1

CONTENTS

INTRODUCTION

Chinese cooking with a wok is light, fresh, fast and delicious – and easy too, be it stir-frying, steaming or deep-frying. In this book you will find an exciting collection of fifty recipes inspired by the wealth of exotic ingredients imported from all corners of the eastern world – from Japan, India and Southeast Asia as well as China. There are mouth-watering stir-fries, sensational soups and salads, tasty noodle dishes and spicy curries, all beautifully illustrated in color with step-by-step instructions.

The sections on ingredients, techniques and equipment are brimming with advice and will arm you with the know-how to make the most of your wok. The ingredients used throughout the book are generally available at large supermarkets and Asian grocers. Don't be put off by any of the more unusual ingredients – these add an authentic note to the recipes and, in many cases, a unique flavor and aroma. Because cooking times are short, the emphasis is on quality and freshness. Cuts of meat should be lean and tender and vegetables and herbs bright and fresh.

I hope that the recipes which follow will give you an insight into the wok's versatility and that you too become devoted to this method of cooking, leaving your saucepans and frying pans on the kitchen shelf!

Herbs, Spices and Flavorings

Basil
Several different types of basil are used in Asian cooking. Thai cooks use two varieties, holy and sweet basil, but ordinary basil works well in the recipes in this book.

Cardamom
Available both as tiny green pods and large black pods containing seeds, cardamom has a strong aromatic quality. For the recipes in this book, use the green ones either whole and lightly crushed or, if you want a more intense flavor, remove the seeds and discard the pods.

Cashew Nuts
Whole cashew nuts feature prominently in Chinese stir-fries, especially those with chicken.

Chilies
There is a wide range of fresh and dried chilies from which to choose. Generally the larger the chili, the milder the flavor, but there are some exceptions, and the only way to gauge potency is by taste. Remove the seeds for a milder flavor. Whether using dried or fresh chilies, take care when preparing them as their seeds and flesh can "burn".

Chili Oil
A red flavoring oil, sometimes containing chili flakes. Use this oil sparingly.

Chinese Five-spice Powder
A distinctive Chinese flavoring containing star anise, pepper, fennel, cloves and cinnamon.

Chinese Rice Vinegar
Chinese white rice vinegar can sometimes be difficult to find outside Chinese supermarkets. If you cannot find it, use cider vinegar instead.

Chinese Rice Wine
Shaohsing wine is reputedly the finest variety. It has a rich sherry-like flavor and can be found in most larger supermarkets and Asian grocers.

Cilantro/Coriander
Widely used in wok cookery, the fresh herb is called cilantro. If the leaves are torn rather than chopped, the flavor is more subtle. Ground coriander, made from dried seeds, tastes completely different from the fresh herb: it has a fairly mild, slightly musky flavor.

Coconut
Coconut milk is used extensively in wok cookery, particularly in Thai curries. It can be freshly made or bought in cans, or you can use powdered or creamed coconut sold in blocks, and reconstitute them with water. Dried grated coconut flakes, available from health-food stores, makes an excellent garnish.

Cumin
Cumin has a strong, slightly bitter flavor and is used to flavor many Asian dishes.

Dried Shrimps and Dried Shrimp Paste
Dried shrimps are tiny shrimps that are salted and dried. They are used as a seasoning for stir-fried dishes. Soak them first in warm water until soft, then either process them in a blender or food processor or pound them in a mortar with a pestle. Shrimp paste is a dark odorous paste made from fermented shrimps. Use sparingly.

Galangal (Kah, Laos)
Fresh galangal tastes and looks a little like ginger with a pinkish tinge to its skin, however, it is a lot less pungent and more aromatic. It is also available dried and ground.

Garlic
One of the most indispensable ingredients in wok cookery for adding flavor. It can also be sliced and stir-fried to sprinkle over dishes as a garnish.

Ginger
Ginger has a very sharp distinctive taste. Choose firm plump pieces with unwrinkled shiny skins.

Hoisin Sauce
This is a thick, dark, brownish-red sauce which is sweet and spicy.

Kaffir Lime Leaves
Used like bay leaves, but to give an aromatic lime flavor to dishes. The fresh leaves are available from Asian stores and can be frozen for future use.

Lemongrass
Lemongrass imparts a mild, sour-sweet, citrus flavor to dishes. You can split and use it whole or use it finely chopped or ground to a paste.

Mirin
A mild, sweet Japanese rice cooking wine.

Oyster Sauce
A salty brown sauce made from boiled oysters and soy sauce.

Peanut Oil
This has a mild nutty flavor. Its ability to be heated to a high temperature makes it perfect for stir-frying and deep-frying.

Peanuts
Used in wok cookery to add flavor and a crunchy texture. The thin red skins of raw peanuts must be removed. To do this, immerse them in boiling water for a few minutes, after which you can easily slip off the skins.

Sake
A strong, powerful, fortified rice wine from Japan.

Salted Black Beans
These salted fermented soy beans are available in cans and packages. Soak before use and check before seasoning a dish because of their salty nature.

Sesame Oil
This is made from toasted sesame seeds. It is very aromatic and is often added to a finished dish in small quantities.

Soy Sauce
A major seasoning ingredient in Asian cooking, this is made from fermented soy beans combined with yeast, salt and sugar. Chinese soy sauce falls into two main categories: light and dark. Japanese soy sauce (*shoyu*) has a slightly sweet and delicate flavor, while in Malaysian cooking *ketjap manis* is used – a sweet soy sauce with a syrupy texture.

Sweet Chili Sauce
A hot, yet sweet sauce made from chilies, vinegar, sugar and salt. Use sparingly in cooking, and also as a dipping sauce.

Szechuan Peppercorns
Red aromatic peppercorns which are best used roasted and ground.

Tamarind
The brown sticky pulp of the bean-like seed pod of the tamarind tree. The pulp is usually diluted with water and strained before use.

Thai Fish Sauce
Called *nam pla* in Thailand, this is used rather like soy sauce.

Top shelf, left to right: *garlic, ginger, lemongrass, dried shrimp, Thai fish sauce, Szechuan peppercorns, sweet chili sauce, ground coriander, galangal, Chinese five-spice powder, green chilies*

Middle shelf, left to right: *dried red chilies, peanuts (skin on), cardamom pods, cashew nuts (in jar), peanuts (skin off), kaffir lime leaves, tamarind, hoisin sauce, salted black beans, chili oil*

Bottom shelf, back row: *sake, Chinese rice vinegar, Chinese rice wine*

Bottom shelf, middle row: *sesame oil, mirin, peanut oil, cilantro, cumin seeds*

Bottom shelf, front: *basil, dried shrimp paste, red & green chilies, flaked coconut & creamed coconut, light soy sauce, oyster sauce, pieces of coconut, whole coconut*

Vegetables and Pantry Ingredients

Most of the vegetables used in this book will be familiar to you, but descriptions of some of the more exotic ones are given below for those who are more adventurous. Remember always to buy the best and freshest vegetables and cook them for only a short time so that they retain their crispness, color and nutrients.

Bak Choy
An attractive vegetable with a long, smooth, milky-white stem and large, dark green leaves.

Bamboo Shoots
These mild-flavored tender shoots of the young bamboo are available fresh in Asian stores, or sliced and halved in cans. Clean thoroughly before use.

Beansprouts
These shoots of the mung bean are usually available from supermarkets. They add a crisp texture to stir-fries.

Canned Corn
Baby corn cobs have a crunchy texture and a mild, sweet flavor and are an attractive ingredient. They are widely available from supermarkets, mostly in canned or bottled form, or frozen.

Chinese Cabbage
Sometimes known as Napa cabbage. It looks like a large, tightly packed Romaine lettuce with firm, pale green, crinkled leaves. It has a delicious crunchy texture.

Chinese Long Beans
These are long thin beans similar to green beans but three or four times longer. Cut into smaller lengths and use just like ordinary green beans.

Chinese Pancakes
These are flour-and-water pancakes with no seasonings or spices added. They are available fresh or frozen; if using frozen pancakes, thaw them thoroughly before steaming them.

Gram Flour
Gram flour is made from ground chickpeas and has a unique flavor. It is well worth seeking out in Indian food stores or health-food stores, but if you prefer you can use plain wholewheat flour instead, adding extra water.

Mushrooms
Both fresh and dried mushrooms can be used in wok cookery to add texture and flavor to a dish. Dried mushrooms need to be soaked in warm water for 20–30 minutes before use. The soaking liquor, once it has been strained, can be used as a stock. Although dried mushrooms are expensive per package, only a few are needed per recipe and they can be stored indefinitely.

Noodles
A wide variety of fresh and dried noodles is available. These can be interchanged in most recipes. Some types of noodles may require quick cooking, while others need soaking in boiling water. They can be made from wheat, rice, ground beans or buckwheat. Follow the cooking instructions on the package.

Rice
For the purposes of this book long-grain white rice is used, varying from Thai jasmine to Indian basmati. Long-grain rices such as patna and basmati tend to be drier and their grains remain separate when cooked; Thai jasmine rice, though delicious, is soft, light and stickier. Directions for cooking rice are in individual recipes.

Scallions
This slender spring onion is the immature bulb of the yellow onion. When recipes refer to the "white" part this is the firm, mainly white section which makes up most of the onion; "green" is the leaves.

Shallots
Shallots are small mild-flavored members of the onion family with copper-red skins. They can be used in the same way as onions or ground into Thai curry pastes or fried into crisp flakes to be used as a garnish.

Snow Peas
These tender green peapods, containing flat, barely formed peas, are highly valued for their crisp texture and sweet flavor.

Spring Roll Wrappers
Paper-thin wrappers made from wheat flour or rice flour and water. They are available from most Asian grocers. Wheat flour wrappers are sold frozen and need to be thawed and carefully separated before use. Rice wrappers are dry and must be gently soaked before use.

Tofu
Tofu is also known as bean curd. Blocks of firm tofu are used in the recipes in this book as it is more suitable for stir-frying and deep-frying. Although rather bland in flavor, it readily absorbs the flavors of other ingredients. It can be stored in the fridge for several days covered with water.

Water Chestnuts
A walnut-sized bulb of an Asian water plant that resembles a chestnut with its outer brown layer. Once peeled, the flesh is crisp and sweet. They are sold fresh by some Asian grocers, but are more readily available canned, whole or sliced.

Wonton Wrappers
Paper-thin squares of yellow-colored dough, these are sold in most Asian food stores.

Top shelf, left to right: *egg noodles, wonton wrappers, water chestnuts, cellophane noodles, gram flour, spring roll wrappers*

Middle shelf, left to right: *dried Chinese mushrooms, bok choy, tofu, egg noodles, Chinese pancakes*

Bottom, left to right: *rice, (in basket) snow peas, corn, shallots, shiitake mushrooms, bamboo shoots, beansprouts, Chinese cabbage, scallions, Chinese long beans*

At front: *wood ears (mushrooms)*

Equipment

The equipment required for cooking the recipes in this book is generally simple and inexpensive, especially if you seek out authentic implements from Indian stores.

Bamboo Steamer

For steaming, this fits inside the wok, where it should rest safely perched on the sloping sides. It comes in various sizes, from small for dim sum to those large enough to hold a whole fish.

Bamboo Strainer

A wide, flat, metal strainer with a long bamboo handle which makes lifting of foods from steam or hot oil easier. A metal slotted spoon can be used instead.

Chopsticks

Long wooden chopsticks are useful for stirring, fluffing up rice, separating noodles during cooking and turning and transferring items.

Cleaver

This all-purpose cutting tool is available in various weights and sizes. It is easy to use and serves many purposes, from chopping up bones to precision cutting, like deveining shrimp.

Grater

Chinese graters are typically wooden.

Kadhai

Most kadhai recipes are very simple to prepare and need very little equipment. A lot of dishes are cooked and served in one pan called a kadhai, or karahi. This is to kadhai cooking what the wok is to Chinese cooking.

It is a round-bottomed pan with two handles used for stir-frying, braising and deep-frying.

The kadhai pan is not essential for the recipes in this book: a wok or frying pan can be used instead, although the latter lacks the authenticity which is part of the fun.

The wok has a number of accessories that work just as well with the kadhai – a wok stand helps to keep it steady during deep-frying, a wok scoop/spatula is shaped to fit the curves of the pan and a well-fitting domed lid can be used when braising. Like the wok a new kadhai needs to be seasoned and allowed to take on the blackened patina that builds up over time, and which is said to improve the flavor of the food being cooked. Kadhais can be bought at Asian supermarkets.

The Wok

Many varieties of wok are available, and while the term wok applies specifically to a Chinese cooking vessel, most Asian cooks use a version of this pan. The wok and its cousins are bowl-shaped with gently sloping sides which allow the heat to spread rapidly and evenly over the surface, thus making for rapid cooking which is fundamental to stir-frying. The wok's large capacity also makes it excellent for deep-frying, steaming and braising, although

care must be taken to keep it steady during these operations. The available woks may have ear-shaped handles of metal or wood, a single long handle or both for you to choose from.

Choosing a Wok

Choose a wok about 14 in in diameter with good deep sides – this will be large enough for most recipes but not so large as to be unwieldly. Select one which is heavy and, if possible, made of carbon steel rather than stainless steel which tends to scorch. Cast iron is excellent too, as it is a good conductor of heat. Both metals develop a "non-stick" patina with use. Woks already lined with non-stick finishes are not advisable; not only are they more expensive but they cannot be seasoned like an ordinary wok nor can they withstand the high heat required for wok cooking. A traditional round-bottomed wok works well on a gas burner, but flat-based woks are now available for use on electric burners.

Seasoning a Wok

All new woks except non-stick ones need to be seasoned. Many need to be scrubbed first with a cream cleanser to remove the manufacturer's protective coating of oil. Once the oil has been removed, place the wok over a low heat and add about 2 tbsp vegetable oil. Using a pad of paper towels, rub the entire inside of the wok with the oil. Heat the wok slowly for 10–15 minutes and then wipe off the oil with more paper towels; the paper will become black. Repeat this process of coating, heating and wiping several times until the paper is clean.

The wok is now seasoned; do not scrub it again. After use, just

wash it in hot water without detergent, then wipe it dry. The wok will rust if not in constant use. If it does, scour the rust off and repeat the seasoning process.

Wok Accessories

There is a range of accessories available to go with woks, although in most cases an adequate substitute may be found in the kitchen.

Wok Brush

This bundle of stiff split bamboo is used for cleaning the wok. It is not essential and any ordinary kitchen brush will do just as well.

Wok Lid

A wok lid is a dome-like cover, usually made of aluminium, which is used for steaming and braising. It may come with the wok or be purchased separately, but any domed saucepan lid which fits snugly over the top of the wok can be used instead.

Wok Scoop/Spatula

A long-handled metal spatula with a wooden end used to toss and turn ingredients when stir-frying. Any good long-handled spoon can be used instead, although it does not have quite the same action.

Wok Stand

Used to provide a secure base for the wok when it is used for steaming, braising or deep-frying. Stands are made of metal and are either simple open-sided frames or solid metal rings with holes punched around the sides.

Trivet

If you use your wok to steam, you will need a wooden or metal trivet to stand above the water level and support the plate.

bamboo steamer

trivet

wok brush

wooden spatula

chopsticks

wok scoop

metal spatula

grater

strainer

wok stand and trivet

cleaver

wok

kadhai pan

Preparing Ingredients

While stir-frying is quick and easy, it is essential to know how to prepare ingredients for cooking in order to be successful. Asian cooks always use a cleaver for these tasks, but a sharp heavy knife can be used instead. For the ingredients to cook as quickly as possible and properly absorb the taste of the oil and flavorings despite the short cooking time, they should be cut into small uniform pieces and as many cut surfaces as possible should be exposed to the heat. Another important reason for careful cutting is to enhance the visual appeal of a dish. This is why most Asian cuisines are so specific about cutting techniques, particularly vegetables.

COOK'S TIP
Because ingredients are cooked for the minimum amount of time in a wok, use only the freshest of vegetables and only premium cuts of meat and poultry bought the same day.

VEGETABLES
Some vegetables such as broccoli and cauliflower are cut according to their natural shape into florets; others are sliced, diagonally sliced, shredded, diced or roll cut depending on the dish.

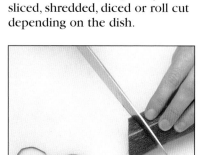

1 Diagonal cutting is a technique used for cutting vegetables such as carrots, asparagus or scallions. It allows more of the surface of the vegetable to be exposed for quicker cooking. Simply angle the cleaver or knife at a slant and cut.

2 Roll cutting is like diagonal cutting but is used for larger vegetables such as zucchini, eggplant or large carrots. Start by making one diagonal slice at one end of the vegetable, then turn it 180° and make the next diagonal cut. Continue until you have cut the entire vegetable into even-size chunks.

MEAT
Meat for stir-frying and sometimes steaming is cut into thin slices, matchstick strips or cubes. This way it can be quickly stir-fried or steamed without losing any of its tenderness.

1 Beef is always cut across the grain, otherwise it would become tough; pork, lamb and chicken can be cut either along or across the grain.

2 Placing the meat in the freezer for about 1 hour beforehand makes it easier to cut paper-thin slices.

CHOPPING HERBS

1 Strip the leaves from the stalks and pile them on a chopping board.

2 Using a cleaver or chef's knife, cut the herbs into small pieces, moving the blade back and forth until the herbs are as coarse or fine as you wish.

PEELING AND CHOPPING LEMONGRASS

1 Cut off and discard the dry leafy tops, leaving about 6 in of stalk. Peel away any tough outer layers from the lemongrass.

2 Lay the lemongrass on a board. Set a cleaver or chef's knife on top and strike it firmly with your fist – this helps to extract maximum flavor. Cut across the lemongrass to make thin slices, then continue chopping until fine.

PREPARING BEANSPROUTS

1 Pick over the beansprouts, discarding any that are discolored, broken or wilted.

2 Rinse the beansprouts under cold running water and drain well.

PREPARING KAFFIR LIME LEAVES

1 Using a small sharp knife, remove the center vein.

2 Cut the leaves crosswise into very fine strips.

PEELING AND CHOPPING GARLIC

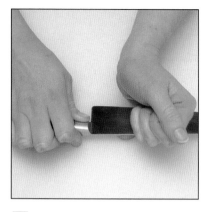

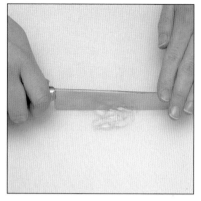

1 Lay the unpeeled garlic clove on a board. Set the flat side of a cleaver or chef's knife on top and strike it firmly with your fist.

2 Peel off and discard the skin. Finely chop the garlic, using the cleaver, moving the blade back and forth.

PEELING AND CHOPPING GINGER

1 Using a small sharp knife, peel the skin from the ginger.

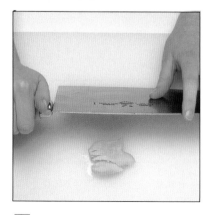

2 Place the ginger on a board. Set the flat side of a cleaver or chef's knife on top and strike it firmly with your fist – this will soften its fibrous texture.

3 Chop the ginger as coarsely or finely as you wish, moving the blade backwards and forwards.

CUTTING AND SHREDDING GARLIC AND GINGER

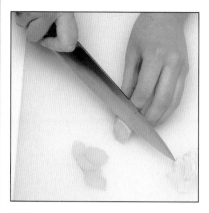

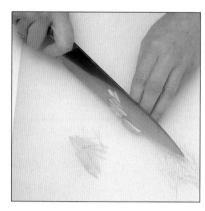

1 Peel the skin from the ginger or garlic clove. Using a cleaver or chef's knife, cut into thin slices.

2 To cut into shreds, arrange the slices one on top of another and cut lengthwise into fine strips.

REMOVING SEEDS FROM CHILIES

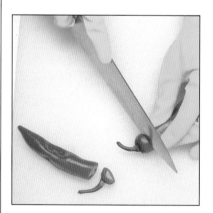

1 Wearing rubber gloves, remove the stalks from chilies.

2 Cut in half lengthwise.

3 Using a small sharp knife, scrape out the seeds and fleshy white ribs from each half.

Garnishes

Many Asian dishes rely on garnishes to add a colorful finishing decorative touch. The garnishes can be simple, such as chopped cilantro, fresh herb sprigs, or finely shredded scallions or chili, or more elaborate, such as cucumber fans, scallion brushes and chili flowers.

CHILI FLOWER

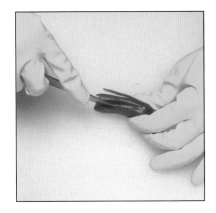

1 Make several lengthwise cuts through a chili from below the stalk to the tip. Remove and discard any seeds.

2 Soak the chili in iced water until the ends curl to form a "flower". Pat dry with paper towels before use.

CUCUMBER FAN

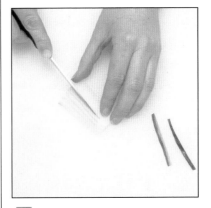   

1 Cut a slice of cucumber lengthwise, about 3 in long, avoiding the seeds. Remove any skin and cut into strips to within ½ in from the end. Remove alternate strips.

2 Carefully bend the strips towards the uncut end, tucking them in so that they stay securely in place. Allow to soak in iced water until required and pat dry before use.

SCALLION BRUSH

1 Trim the green part of a scallion and remove the base of the bulb – you should then be left with a piece about 3 in long. Then make a lengthwise cut approximately 1 in long at one end of the scallion.

2 Roll the scallion through 90° and cut again. Repeat this process at the other end. Place in iced water until the shreds open out and curl. Pat dry with paper towels before use.

Spice Mixtures and Stocks

Use these spice mixtures to add heat and flavor to Thai curries, fish cakes and kadhai dishes. They are quick and easy to make, but you can buy them ready-made from larger supermarkets.

THAI RED CURRY PASTE

INGREDIENTS
4 fresh red chilies
1-in piece fresh ginger
4 shallots
4–6 garlic cloves
4 lemongrass stalks
4 tsp coriander seeds
2 tsp cumin seeds
2 tsp hot paprika
¼ tsp ground turmeric
½ tsp salt
grated rind and juice of 2 limes
1 tbsp vegetable oil

THAI GREEN CURRY PASTE

INGREDIENTS
6 scallions
4 cilantro stems, washed
4 kaffir lime leaves
6–8 fresh green chilies
4 garlic cloves, chopped
1-in piece fresh ginger, chopped
1 lemongrass stalk, chopped
3 tbsp chopped fresh cilantro
3 tbsp chopped fresh basil
1 tbsp vegetable oil

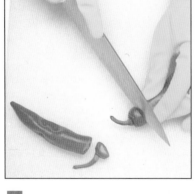

1 Peel and chop the ginger, shallots and garlic. Peel and finely chop the lemongrass. Wearing rubber gloves, remove the stalks from the chilies, then cut them in half lengthwise. Scrape out the seeds and fleshy white ribs, then coarsely chop the flesh.

2 Heat a small frying pan over medium heat, then add the coriander and cumin seeds. Toss them in the pan until the spices turn a shade darker and emit a roasted aroma. Allow to cool.

3 Place all the ingredients in a blender or food processor and process to form a smooth paste. Store in a screw-top jar for up to 1 month in the fridge and use as required.

1 Chop the scallions and cilantro stems. Remove the center vein from the kaffir lime leaves, then cut into fine shreds. Seed and chop the chilies.

2 Put all the ingredients in a blender or food processor and process to form a smooth paste. Store in a screw-top jar for up to 2 weeks in the fridge and use as required.

GARAM MASALA

INGREDIENTS
3-in piece cinnamon stick
2 bay leaves
1 tsp cumin seeds
1 tsp whole cloves
1 tsp black peppercorns
¼ nutmeg, grated

I Break the cinnamon stick into pieces. Crumble the bay leaves.

2 Heat a small frying pan over medium heat, then add the bay leaves and all the spices except the nutmeg. Dry-roast until the spices turn a shade darker and emit a roasted aroma, stirring or shaking the pan frequently to prevent burning. Allow to cool. Place all the ingredients in a spice mill or electric coffee grinder and grind to a fine powder. Store in a small jar with a tight-fitting lid for up to 2 months.

CHICKEN STOCK

INGREDIENTS
2¼ lb uncooked chicken bones,
    such as backs, wings etc.
1¼ lb chicken pieces
10 cups water
2 thin slices fresh ginger
2 scallions, white parts only
2 unpeeled garlic cloves
salt, to taste

I Place all the ingredients except the salt in a large pan and bring to a simmer. Skim off any scum. Simmer for 3–4 hours to extract all the flavor. Season with salt to taste.

2 Strain the stock, pressing the solid ingredients with the back of a ladle or spoon to extract all the liquid. Allow the stock to cool, then chill. Spoon off the fat from the surface. Use as required.

FRESH COCONUT MILK

INGREDIENTS
grated fresh coconut,
    to fill a measuring jug
    to the 1⅔ cups mark
1¼ cups hot water

I First you will need to break open a fresh coconut. To do this, push a skewer into the three holes in the top of the coconut and drain out the liquid. Place the coconut in a plastic bag and hit it hard with a hammer. To remove the outer shell from the coconut pieces, prise the tip of a small sharp knife between it and the coconut flesh. Remove the inner brown skin using a potato peeler. Grate the flesh.

2 Put the measured grated coconut and hot water into a blender or food processor fitted with a metal blade and process for 1 minute. Strain the coconut mixture through a sieve lined with muslin into a bowl, gathering up the corners of the cloth and squeezing out the liquid. The coconut milk is now ready; stir before use.

left to right:
chicken stock
garam masala
fresh coconut
    milk

Cooking Techniques

STIR-FRYING

This quick technique retains the fresh flavor, color and texture of ingredients and its success depends upon having all the required ingredients prepared before cooking.

1 Heat an empty wok over high heat. This prevents food sticking and will ensure an even heat. Add the oil and swirl it around so that it coats the bottom and halfway up the sides of the wok. It is important that the oil is hot enough so that when food is added it will start to cook immediately, but it should not be so hot that it is smoking.

2 Ingredients should then be added in a specific order, usually aromatics first (garlic, ginger, scallions). If this is the case, do not wait for the oil to get so hot that it is almost smoking or they will burn and become bitter. Toss them in the oil for a few seconds. Now add the main ingredients which require longer cooking, such as dense vegetables or meat, followed by the faster-cooking items. Toss and turn the ingredients from the center of the wok to the sides.

DEEP FRYING

A wok is ideal for deep-frying as it uses far less oil than a deep-fat fryer. Make sure, however, that it is fully secure on its stand before adding the oil and never leave the wok unattended.

1 Put the wok on a stand and half-fill with oil. Heat until the required temperature registers on a thermometer. Alternatively, test it by dropping in a small piece of food; if bubbles form all over the surface of the food, the oil is ready.

2 Carefully add the food to the oil using long wooden chopsticks or tongs and move it around to prevent it sticking together. Using a bamboo strainer or slotted spoon, carefully remove the food and drain on paper towels before serving.

STEAMING

Steamed foods are cooked by a gentle moist heat which must circulate freely in order for the food to cook. Increasingly popular with health conscious cooks, steaming preserves flavor and nutrients. It is perfect for vegetables, meat, poultry and especially fish. The easiest way to steam in a wok is with a bamboo steamer but you can do without.

USING A BAMBOO STEAMER IN A WOK

1 Put the wok on a stand. Pour about 2 in water into the wok and bring to simmering point. Put the bamboo steamer containing the food into the wok, where it will rest on the sloping sides.

2 Cover the steamer with its matching lid and steam for the recommended time. Check the water level occasionally and add with boiling water as necessary.

USING A WOK AS A STEAMER

1 Place a trivet in the wok, then place the wok on its stand on the burner. Pour in enough boiling water to come just below the trivet, then carefully place the plate holding whatever is to be steamed on the trivet.

2 Cover the wok with its lid, bring to a boil, then lower the heat to a gentle simmer. Steam for the recommended time, checking the water level occasionally and adding with boiling water as necessary.

Lettuce-wrapped Garlic Lamb

This tasty first course lamb is stir-fried with garlic, ginger and spices, then served in crisp lettuce leaves with yogurt, a dab of lime pickle and mint leaves – the contrast of hot and spicy and cool and crisp is excellent.

Serves 4

INGREDIENTS
1 lb lamb, shoulder cutlet
½ tsp cayenne pepper
2 tsp ground coriander
1 tsp ground cumin
½ tsp ground turmeric
2 tbsp peanut oil
3–4 garlic cloves,
    chopped
1 tbsp grated fresh ginger
⅔ cup lamb stock or
    water
4–6 scallions, sliced
2 tbsp chopped fresh
    cilantro
15 ml/1 tbsp lemon juice
lettuce leaves, yogurt, lime pickle
    and mint leaves, to serve

cilantro

stock

garlic

lamb

ginger

peanut oil

scallions

VARIATION
Vegetables, such as cooked diced potatoes or peas, can be added to the ground lamb mixture.

1 Trim the lamb cutlet of any fat and cube into small pieces, then grind in a blender or food processor, taking care not to over-process.

2 In a bowl mix together the cayenne pepper, ground coriander, cumin and turmeric. Add the lamb and rub the spice mixture into the meat. Cover and let marinate for about 1 hour.

3 Heat a wok until hot. Add the oil and swirl it around. When hot, add the garlic and ginger and allow to sizzle for a few seconds.

4 Add the lamb and continue to stir-fry for 2–3 minutes.

5 Pour in the stock and continue to stir-fry until all the stock has been absorbed and the lamb is tender, adding more stock if necessary.

6 Add the scallions, fresh cilantro and lemon juice, then stir-fry for another 30–45 seconds. Serve at once with the lettuce leaves, yogurt, pickle and mint leaves.

Crispy "Seaweed" with Flaked Almonds

This popular appetizer in Chinese restaurants is in fact usually made not with seaweed but spring greens such as collard or chard! It is easy to make at home.

Serves 4-6

INGREDIENTS
1 lb spring greens
peanut oil, for deep-frying
¼ tsp sea salt flakes
1 tsp caster sugar
½ cup flaked almonds,
   toasted

spring greens

almonds

peanut oil

sea salt

sugar

COOK'S TIP
It is important to dry the spring greens thoroughly before deep-frying them, otherwise it will be difficult to achieve the desired crispness without destroying their vivid color.

1 Wash the spring greens under cold running water and then pat well with paper towels to dry thoroughly. Remove and discard the thick white stalks from the greens.

2 Lay several leaves on top of one another, roll up tightly and, using a sharp knife, slice as finely as possible into thread-like strips.

3 Half-fill a wok with oil and heat to 350°F. Deep-fry the greens in batches for about 1 minute until they darken and crisp. Remove each batch from the wok as soon as it is ready and drain on paper towels.

4 Transfer the "seaweed" to a serving dish, sprinkle with the salt and sugar, then mix well. Garnish with the toasted flaked almonds sprinkled over.

Thai Fish Cakes

Bursting with the flavors of chilies, lime and lemongrass, these little fish cakes make a wonderful appetizer.

Serves 4

INGREDIENTS
1 lb white fish fillets, such as
    cod or haddock
3 scallions, sliced
2 tbsp chopped fresh cilantro
2 tbsp Thai red curry paste
1 fresh green chili,
    seeded and chopped
2 tsp grated lime rind
1 tbsp lime juice
2 tbsp peanut oil
salt, to taste
crisp lettuce leaves,
    shredded scallions,
    fresh red chili slices,
    cilantro sprigs and
    lime wedges, to serve

lettuce   *white fish fillets*

lime   *scallions*

peanut oil

cilantro

red chilli

green chili   *Thai red curry paste*

1 Cut the fish into chunks, then place in a blender or food processor.

2 Add the scallions, cilantro, red curry paste, green chili, lime rind and juice to the fish. Season with salt. Process until finely ground.

3 Using lightly floured hands, divide the mixture into 16 pieces and shape each one into a small cake about 1½ in across. Place the fish cakes on a plate, cover with plastic wrap and chill for about 2 hours, until firm. Heat the wok over high heat until hot. Add the oil and swirl it around.

4 Fry the fish cakes, a few at a time, for 6–8 minutes, turning them carefully until evenly browned. Drain each batch on paper towels and keep hot while cooking the remainder. Serve on a bed of crisp lettuce leaves with shredded scallions, red chili slices, cilantro sprigs and lime wedges.

Chinese Spiced Salt Spareribs

Fragrant with spices, this authentic Chinese dish makes a great beginning to an informal meal. Don't forget the finger bowls!

Serves 4

INGREDIENTS
1½–2 lb meaty pork spareribs
1½ tbsp cornstarch
peanut oil, for deep frying
cilantro sprigs, to garnish

FOR THE SPICED SALT
1 tsp Szechuan peppercorns
2 tbsp coarse sea salt
½ tsp Chinese five-
　spice powder

FOR THE MARINADE
2 tbsp light soy sauce
1 tsp caster sugar
1 tbsp Chinese rice wine
ground black pepper

Chinese rice wine

pork spareribs

Chinese five-spice powder

Szechuan peppercorns

cilantro

light soy sauce

peanut oil

sea salt

1 Using a heavy sharp cleaver, chop the spareribs into pieces about 2 in long or ask your butcher to do this, then place them in a shallow dish.

2 To make the spiced salt, heat a wok to medium heat. Add the Szechuan peppercorns and salt and dry-fry for about 3 minutes, stirring constantly, until the mixture colors slightly. Remove from the heat and stir in the five-spice powder. Allow to cool.

3 Using a mortar and pestle or an electric coffee grinder, grind the spiced salt to a fine powder.

4 Sprinkle 1 tsp of the spiced salt over the spareribs and rub in well with your hands. Add the soy sauce, sugar, rice wine or sherry and some freshly ground black pepper, then toss the ribs in the marinade until well coated. Cover and allow to marinate in the fridge for about 2 hours, turning the spareribs occasionally.

COOK'S TIP

Any leftover spiced salt can be kept for several months in a screw-top jar. Use to rub on the flesh of duck, chicken or pork before cooking.

5 Pour off any excess marinade from the spareribs. Sprinkle the pieces with cornstarch and mix well to coat evenly.

6 Half-fill a wok with oil and heat to 350°F. Deep-fry the spareribs in batches for 3 minutes, until pale golden. Remove and set aside. Reheat the oil to the same temperature. Return the spareribs to the oil and deep-fry for a second time for 1–2 minutes, until crisp and thoroughly cooked. Drain on paper towels. Transfer the ribs to a warmed serving platter and sprinkle over 1–1½ tsp spiced salt. Garnish with cilantro sprigs.

Steamed Spiced Pork and Water Chestnut Wontons

Ginger and Chinese five-spice powder flavor this version of steamed open dumplings – a favorite snack in many teahouses.

VARIATION

These can also be deep fried, in which case fold the edges over the filling to enclose it completely. Press well to seal. Deep-fry in batches in hot oil for about 2 minutes.

Makes about 36

INGREDIENTS
2 large Chinese cabbage leaves, plus extra for lining the steamer
2 scallions, finely chopped
½-in piece fresh ginger, finely chopped
2 oz canned water chestnuts (drained weight), rinsed and finely chopped
8oz ground pork
½ tsp Chinese five-spice powder
1 tbsp cornstarch
1 tbsp light soy sauce
1 tbsp Chinese rice wine
2 tsp sesame oil
generous pinch of sugar
about 36 wonton wrappers, each 3 in square
light soy sauce and hot chili oil, for dipping

caster sugar

Chinese cabbage

scallions

light soy sauce

sesame oil

cornstarch

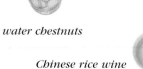
water chestnuts

pork

wonton wrappers

Chinese five-spice powder

Chinese rice wine

ginger

1 Place the Chinese cabbage leaves one on top of another. Cut them lengthwise into quarters and then across into thin shreds.

2 Place the shredded Chinese cabbage leaves in a bowl. Add the scallions, ginger, water chestnuts, pork, five-spice powder, cornstarch, soy sauce, rice wine, sesame oil and sugar; mix well.

3 Set one wonton wrapper on a work surface. Place a heaped teaspoon of the filling in the center of the wrapper, then lightly dampen the edges with water.

4 Lift the wrapper up around the filling, gathering to form a purse. Squeeze the wrapper firmly around the middle, then tap on the bottom to make a flat base. The top should be open. Place the wonton on a tray and cover with a damp dish towel.

5 Line the steamer with cabbage leaves and steam the dumplings for 12–15 minutes or until tender. Remove each batch from the steamer as soon as they are cooked, cover with foil and keep warm. Serve hot with soy sauce and chili oil for dipping.

Vegetable Tempura

These deep-fried fritters are based on Kaki-age, a Japanese dish that often incorporates fish and shrimp as well as vegetables.

Makes 8

INGREDIENTS
2 medium zucchini
½ medium eggplant
1 large carrot
½ small Spanish onion
1 egg
½ cup ice water
1 cup all-purpose flour
salt and ground black pepper
vegetable oil,
    for deep-frying
sea salt flakes, lemon slices and
    Japanese soy sauce (*shoyu*),
    to serve

zucchini

carrot

eggplant

Spanish onion

all-purpose flour

egg

vegetable oil

COOK'S TIP
Paring strips of peel from the zucchini and eggplant will avoid too much tough skin in the finished dish.

1 Using a potato peeler, pare strips of peel from the zucchini and eggplant to give a striped effect.

2 Cut the zucchini, eggplant and carrot into strips about 3–4 in long and ⅛ in wide.

3 Put the zucchini, eggplant and carrot in a colander and sprinkle liberally with salt. Let stand for about 30 minutes, then rinse thoroughly under cold running water. Drain well.

4 Thinly slice the onion from top to base, discarding the plump pieces in the middle. Separate the layers so that there are lots of fine long strips. Mix all the vegetables together and season with salt and pepper.

5 Make the batter immediately before frying: mix the egg and iced water in a bowl, then sift in the flour. Mix very briefly using a fork or chopsticks. Do not overmix – the batter should remain lumpy. Add the vegetables to the batter and mix to combine.

6 Meanwhile, half-fill a wok with oil and heat to 350°F. Scoop up one heaped tablespoon of the mixture at a time and carefully lower into the oil. Deep-fry in batches for about 3 minutes, until golden brown and crisp. Drain on paper towels. Serve each diner with salt, lemon slices and a tiny bowl of Japanese soy sauce for dipping.

Hot Spicy Crab Claws

Crab claws are used to delicious effect in this quick appetizer based on an Indonesian dish called *Kepiting Pedas*.

Serves 4

INGREDIENTS

12 fresh or frozen and thawed
    cooked crab claws
4 shallots, coarsely chopped
2–4 fresh red chilies, seeded and
    coarsely chopped
3 garlic cloves, coarsely chopped
1 tsp grated fresh ginger
½ tsp ground coriander
3 tbsp peanut oil
60 ml/4 tbsp water
10 ml/2 tsp sweet soy sauce
    (*kecap manis*)
2–3 tsp lime juice
salt, to taste
fresh coriander, to garnish

shallots

crab claws

sweet soy sauce

garlic

coriander

red chilies

peanut oil

lime

ginger

1 Crack the crab claws with the back of a heavy knife to make eating easier. Set aside. In a mortar, pound the chopped shallots with the pestle until pulpy. Add the chilies, garlic, ginger and ground coriander and pound until the mixture forms a coarse paste.

2 Heat the wok over medium heat. Add the oil and swirl it around. When it is hot, stir in the chili paste. Stir-fry for about 30 seconds. Increase the heat to high. Add the crab claws and stir-fry for another 3–4 minutes.

3 Stir in the water, sweet soy sauce, lime juice and salt to taste. Continue to stir-fry for 1–2 minutes. Serve at once, garnished with fresh cilantro. The crab claws are eaten with the fingers, so provide finger bowls.

COOK'S TIP

If whole crab claws are unavailable, look out for frozen prepared crab claws. These are shelled with just the tip of the claw attached to the white meat. Stir-fry for about two minutes until heated through.

Corn and Chicken Soup

This popular classic Chinese soup is delicious, and very easy to make.

Serves 4-6

INGREDIENTS

1 chicken breast fillet,
 about 4 oz, cubed
2 tsp light soy sauce
1 tbsp Chinese rice wine
1 tsp cornstarch
4 tbsp cold water
1 tsp sesame oil
2 tbsp peanut oil
1 tsp fresh ginger,
 finely grated
4 cups chicken stock, or
 bouillon cube and water
15-oz can cream-style corn
8-oz can corn kernels
2 eggs, beaten
2–3 scallions, green parts only,
 cut into tiny rounds
salt and ground black pepper

cornstarch

chicken stock

cream-style corn

chicken

corn kernels

Chinese rice wine

egg

sesame oil

ginger

1 Grind the chicken in a food processor, taking care not to over-process. Transfer the chicken to a bowl and stir in the soy sauce, rice wine, cornstarch, water, sesame oil and seasoning. Cover and leave for about 15 minutes to absorb the flavors.

2 Heat a wok over medium heat. Add the peanut oil and swirl it around. Add the ginger and stir-fry for a few seconds. Add the stock, creamed corn and corn kernels. Bring to just below boiling point.

3 Spoon about 6 tbsp of the hot liquid into the chicken mixture and stir until it forms a smooth paste. Return this to the wok. Slowly bring to a boil, stirring constantly, then simmer for 2–3 minutes until the chicken is cooked.

4 Pour the beaten eggs into the soup in a slow steady stream, using a fork or chopsticks to stir the top of the soup in a figure-eight pattern. The egg should set in lacy shreds. Serve immediately with the scallions sprinkled over.

Crispy Spring Rolls with Sweet Chili Dipping Sauce

Miniature spring rolls make delicious appetizers or party finger food.

Makes 20-24

INGREDIENTS

1 oz rice vermicelli noodles
peanut oil
1 tsp fresh ginger,
  finely grated
2 scallions, finely shredded
2 oz carrot, finely shredded
2 oz snow peas, shredded
1 oz young spinach leaves
2 oz fresh beansprouts
1 tbsp fresh mint,
  finely chopped
1 tbsp fresh cilantro,
  finely chopped
2 tbsp Thai fish sauce (*nam pla*)
20-24 spring roll wrappers,
  each 5 in square
1 egg white, lightly beaten

FOR THE DIPPING SAUCE

4 tbsp sugar
¼ cup rice vinegar
2 fresh red chilies, seeded and
  finely chopped

noodles

spinach

scallions

spring roll wrappers

Thai fish sauce

snow peas

ginger

beansprouts

carrot

COOK'S TIP
You can cook the spring rolls for 2-3 hours in advance, then all you have to do is reheat them on a foil-lined baking sheet at 400°F for about 10 minutes.

1 First make the dipping sauce: place the sugar and vinegar in a small pan with 2 tbsp water. Heat gently, stirring until the sugar dissolves, then boil rapidly until it forms a light syrup. Stir in the chilies and leave to cool.

2 Soak the noodles according to the package instructions; rinse and drain well. Using scissors, snip the noodles into short lengths.

3 Heat a wok until hot. Add 1 tbsp oil and swirl it around. Add the ginger and scallions and stir-fry for 15 seconds. Add the carrot and snow peas and stir-fry for 2–3 minutes. Add the spinach, beansprouts, mint, cilantro, fish sauce and noodles and stir-fry for another minute. Set aside to cool.

4 Take one spring roll wrapper and arrange it so that it faces you in a diamond shape. Place a spoonful of filling just below the center, then fold up the bottom point over the filling.

5 Fold in each side, then roll up tightly. Brush the end with beaten egg white to seal. Repeat until all the filling has been used.

6 Half-fill a wok with oil and heat to 350°F. Deep-fry the spring rolls in batches for 3–4 minutes, until golden and crisp. Drain on paper towels. Serve hot with the sweet chili dipping sauce.

Quick-fried Shrimp with Hot Spices

These spicy shrimp that cook in moments make a wonderful appetizer. Don't forget to provide your guests with finger bowls.

COOK'S TIP
If raw shrimp are unavailable, use cooked ones instead, but simmer gently in the coconut milk for just 1–2 minutes.

Serves 4

INGREDIENTS
1 lb large raw shrimp
1-in piece fresh ginger, grated
2 garlic cloves, crushed
1 tsp cayenne pepper
1 tsp ground turmeric
2 tsp black mustard seeds
seeds from 4 green cardamom pods, crushed
4 tbsp ghee or butter
½ cup coconut milk
2–3 tbsp chopped fresh cilantro
salt and ground black pepper
nan bread, to serve

shrimp

coconut milk

cilantro

cayenne

ghee

black mustard seeds

turmeric

ginger

garlic

cardamom pods

 Peel the shrimp carefully, leaving the tails attached.

 Using a small sharp knife, make a slit along the back of each shrimp and remove the dark vein. Rinse under cold running water, drain and pat dry.

 Put the ginger, garlic, cayenne pepper, turmeric, mustard seeds and cardamom seeds in a bowl. Add the shrimp and toss to coat with the spices.

 Heat a karahi or wok until hot. Add the ghee or butter and swirl it around until foaming.

Add the marinated shrimp and stir-fry for 1–1½ minutes, until they are just turning pink.

Stir in the coconut milk and simmer for 3–4 minutes, until the shrimp are cooked through. Season with salt and pepper. Sprinkle over the cilantro and serve at once with nan bread.

Thai Seafood Salad

This seafood salad with chili, lemongrass and fish sauce is light and refreshing.

Serves 4

INGREDIENTS
8 oz cleaned squid
8 oz raw large shrimp
8 sea scallops, whole
8 oz firm white fish
2–3 tbsp olive oil
small mixed lettuce leaves and
    cilantro sprigs, to serve

FOR THE DRESSING
2 small fresh red chilies, seeded
    and finely chopped
2-in piece lemongrass,
    finely chopped
2 fresh kaffir lime leaves,
    shredded
2 tbsp Thai fish sauce
    (*nam pla*)
2 shallots, thinly sliced
2 tbsp lime juice
2 tbsp rice vinegar
2 tsp sugar

white fish   *squid*

scallops

large shrimp

lemongrass

Thai fish sauce

shallots   *kaffir lime leaves*

1   Prepare the seafood: slit open the squid bodies, score the flesh with a sharp knife, then cut into square pieces. Halve the tentacles, if necessary. Peel and devein the shrimp. Cut the sea scallops in half (if using bay scallops, leave whole). Cube the white fish.

2   Heat a wok until hot. Add the oil and swirl it around, then add the shrimp and stir-fry for 2–3 minutes until pink. Transfer to a large bowl. Stir-fry the squid and scallops for 1–2 minutes, until opaque. Remove and add to the shrimp. Stir-fry the white fish for 2–3 minutes. Remove and add to the cooked seafood. Reserve any juices.

3   Put all the dressing ingredients in a small bowl with the reserved juices from the wok; mix well.

4   Pour the dressing over the seafood and toss gently. Arrange the salad leaves and cilantro sprigs on four individual plates, then spoon the seafood on top. Serve at once.

Spicy Fish Fritters

These crispy, spicy fritters are based on a dish from Baltistan, India.

Serves 4

INGREDIENTS

2 tsp cumin seeds
2 tsp coriander seeds
1–2 dried red chilies
2 tbsp vegetable oil
1½ cups gram flour
1 tsp salt
2 tsp garam masala
1 cup water
peanut oil, for deep-frying
1½ lb fish fillets, such as cod, skinned, boned and cut into thick strips
mint sprigs and lime halves, to garnish

fish fillets

peanut oil

gram flour

red chilies

vegetable oil

coriander   *garam masala*

1 Crush the cumin, coriander and chili(es), using a mortar and pestle. Heat the vegetable oil in a kadhai or wok and stir-fry the spices for 1–2 minutes.

2 Put the gram flour, salt, spice mixture and garam masala in a bowl. Gradually stir in enough water to make a thick batter. Cover and allow to rest for 30 minutes.

3 Half-fill a kadhai or wok with peanut oil and heat to 375°F. When the oil is ready, dip the fish, just a few pieces at a time, into the batter, shaking off any excess.

4 Deep-fry the fish in batches for 4–5 minutes, until golden brown. Drain on paper towels. Serve immediately, garnished with mint sprigs and lime halves for squeezing over the fritters.

Fish Balls with Chinese Greens

These tasty fish balls are easy to make using a food processor. Here they are partnered with a selection of green vegetables – bok choy is available at most Asian stores.

Serves 4

INGREDIENTS
FOR THE FISH BALLS
1 lb white fish fillets, skinned,
    boned and cubed
3 scallions, chopped
1 slice Canadian bacon,
    rinded and chopped
1 tbsp Chinese rice wine
2 tbsp light soy sauce
1 egg white

FOR THE VEGETABLES
1 small head bok choy
1 tsp cornstarch
1 tbsp light soy sauce
⅔ cup fish stock
2 tbsp peanut oil
2 garlic cloves, sliced
1-in piece fresh ginger,
    cut into thin shreds
3 oz green beans
6 oz snow peas
3 scallions, sliced diagonally
    into 2–3-in lengths
salt and ground black pepper

garlic   ginger

scallions

bacon

light soy sauce

bok choy

snow peas

green beans   fish stock

fish fillets

Chinese rice wine   peanut oil

1 Put the fish, scallions, bacon, rice wine, soy sauce and egg white in a food processor. Process until smooth. With wetted hands, form the mixture into about 24 small balls.

2 Steam the fish balls in batches in a lightly greased bamboo steamer in a wok for 5–10 minutes until firm. Remove from the steamer and keep warm.

3 Meanwhile, trim the bok choy, removing any discolored leaves or damaged stems, then tear into manageable pieces.

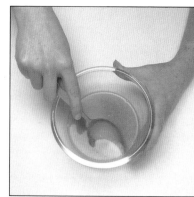

4 In a small bowl blend together the cornstarch, soy sauce and stock.

VARIATION
Replace the snow peas and green beans with broccoli florets. Blanch them before stir-frying.

5 Heat a wok until hot, add the oil and swirl it around. Add the garlic and ginger and stir-fry for 1 minute. Add the beans and stir-fry for 2–3 minutes, then add the snow peas, scallions and pak choi. Stir-fry for 2–3 minutes.

6 Add the sauce to the wok and cook, stirring, until it has thickened and the vegetables are tender but crisp. Taste and adjust the seasoning, if necessary. Serve at once with the fish balls.

Red Snapper with Ginger and Scallions

This is a classic Chinese way of cooking fish. Pouring the oil slowly over the scallions and ginger allows it to partially cook them, enhancing their flavor.

Serves 2-3

INGREDIENTS
1 red snapper, about
   1½-2 lb, cleaned and scaled
   with head left on
1 bunch scallions, cut into thin
   shreds
1-in piece fresh ginger, cut into
   thin shreds
¼ tsp salt
¼ tsp sugar
3 tbsp peanut oil
1 tsp sesame oil
2-3 tbsp light soy sauce
scallion brushes, to garnish

scallions

ginger

peanut oil

sesame oil

red snapper

light soy sauce

sugar

COOK'S TIP
If the fish is too big to fit inside the steamer, cut off the head and place it alongside the body, which can then be reassembled after it is cooked for serving.

1   Rinse the fish, then pat dry with paper towels. Slash the flesh diagonally, three times on each side. Set the fish on a heatproof oval plate that will fit inside your bamboo steamer.

2   Tuck about one-third of the scallions and ginger inside the body cavity. Place the plate inside the steamer, cover with its lid, then place in a wok.

3   Steam over medium heat for 10–15 minutes, until the fish flakes easily when tested with the tip of a knife.

4   Carefully remove the plate from the steamer. Sprinkle over the salt, sugar and remaining scallions and ginger.

5   Heat the oils in a small pan until very hot, then slowly pour over the fish.

6   Drizzle over the soy sauce and serve at once, garnished with scallion brushes.

Sweet-and-sour Fish

The combination of sweet and sour is a popular
one in many cuisines. The sauce can be made up to
two days in advance.

Serves 3–4

INGREDIENTS
1 lb white fish fillets, skinned,
  boned and cubed
½ tsp Chinese five-spice
  powder
1 tsp light soy sauce
1 egg, lightly beaten
2–3 tbsp cornstarch
peanut oil, for deep-frying

FOR THE SAUCE
2 tsp cornstarch
4 tbsp water
4 tbsp pineapple juice
3 tbsp Chinese rice vinegar
3 tbsp sugar
2 tsp light soy sauce
2 tbsp tomato ketchup
2 tsp Chinese rice wine or
  medium-dry sherry
3 tbsp peanut oil
1 garlic clove, crushed
1 tbsp finely chopped
  fresh ginger
6 scallions, sliced diagonally
  into 2-in lengths
1 green bell pepper, seeded and
  cut into ¾-in pieces
4 oz fresh pineapple,
  cut into ¾-in pieces
salt and ground black pepper

light soy sauce

white fish

scallion

garlic

cornstarch

egg

green pepper

Chinese rice wine

ginger

Chinese five-spice powder

pineapple

tomato ketchup

COOK'S TIP
When buying the fish for this
dish, select fillets which are ¾ in
or more thick.

1 Put the fish in a bowl. Sprinkle over
the five-spice powder and soy sauce,
then toss gently. Cover and allow to
marinate for about 30 minutes. Dip the
fish in the egg, then in the cornstarch,
shaking off any excess.

2 Half-fill a wok with oil and heat to
375°F. Deep-fry the fish in batches for
about 2 minutes, until golden. Drain and
keep warm. Carefully pour off all the oil
from the wok and wipe clean.

3 To make the sauce, blend together
in a bowl the cornstarch, water,
pineapple juice, rice vinegar, sugar, soy
sauce, ketchup and rice wine or sherry.
Mix well, then set aside.

4 Heat the wok until hot, add 2 tbsp
of the oil and swirl it around. Add the
garlic and ginger and stir-fry for a few
seconds. Add the scallions and green
pepper and stir-fry over medium heat
for 2 minutes. Add the pineapple.

5 Pour in the sauce and cook, stirring
until thickened. Stir in the remaining
1 tbsp oil and add seasoning to taste.
Pour the sauce over the fish and serve
at once.

Green Seafood Curry

This curry is based on a Thai classic. The lovely green color is imparted by the finely chopped chili and fresh herbs added during the last few moments of cooking.

COOK'S TIP
If you like more fiery curries, increase the amount of green curry paste used.

Serves 4

INGREDIENTS
8 oz small, cleaned squid
8 oz raw large shrimp
1¾ cups coconut milk
2 tbsp green curry paste
2 fresh kaffir lime leaves,
    finely shredded
2 tbsp Thai fish sauce
    (*nam pla*)
1 lb firm white fish fillets,
    skinned, boned and cut
    into chunks
2 fresh green chilies, seeded
    and finely chopped
2 tbsp torn basil or
    cilantro leaves
squeeze of lime juice
Thai jasmine rice, to serve

shrimp

green chilies

squid

white fish

basil

coconut milk

green curry paste

kaffir lime leaves

1 Rinse the squid and pat dry with paper towels. Cut the bodies into rings and halve the tentacles, if necessary.

2 Heat a wok until hot, add the shrimp and stir-fry without any oil for about 4 minutes, until they turn pink.

3 Remove the shrimp from the heat and when they are cool enough to handle, peel off the shells. Make a slit along the back of each one and remove the black vein.

4 Pour the coconut milk into the wok, then bring to a boil, stirring. Add the curry paste, shredded lime leaves and fish sauce. Reduce the heat to a simmer and cook for about 10 minutes, enough for the flavors to develop.

5 Add the squid, shrimp and white fish and cook for about 2 minutes until the seafood is tender. Take care not to overcook the squid, as it will become tough very quickly.

6 Just before serving, stir in the chilies and basil or cilantro. Taste and adjust the flavor with a squeeze of lime juice. Serve with Thai jasmine rice.

Squid with Peppers in Black Bean Sauce

Salted black beans add a traditionally Chinese flavor to this tasty stir-fry.

Serves 4

INGREDIENTS

2 tbsp salted black beans
2 tbsp medium-dry sherry
1 tbsp light soy sauce
1 tsp cornstarch
½ tsp sugar
2 tbsp water
3 tbsp peanut oil
1 lb cleaned squid, scored and
  cut into thick strips
1 tsp finely chopped
  fresh ginger
1 garlic clove, finely chopped
1 fresh green chili,
  seeded and sliced
6–8 scallions, cut diagonally
  into 1-in lengths
½ red and ½ green bell pepper,
  cored seeded and cut into
  1-in diamonds
3 oz shiitake mushrooms,
  thickly sliced

scallions

shiitake mushrooms

medium-dry sherry

light soy sauce

ginger

red pepper

squid

salted black beans   *green pepper*   *green chili*

1 Rinse and finely chop the black beans. Place them in a bowl with the sherry, soy sauce, cornstarch, sugar and water; mix well.

2 Heat a wok until hot, add the oil and swirl it around. When the oil is very hot, add the squid and stir-fry for 1–1½ minutes, until opaque and curled at the edges. Remove with a slotted spoon and set aside.

3 Add the ginger, garlic and chili to the wok and stir-fry for a few seconds. Then add the scallions, peppers and mushrooms, then stir-fry for 2 minutes.

4 Return the squid to the wok with the sauce. Cook, stirring, for about 1 minute, until thickened. Serve at once.

Spiced Scallops in their Shells

Scallops are excellent steamed. When served with this spicy sauce, they make a delicious yet simple appetizer. Each person spoons sauce onto the scallops before eating them.

Serves 4

INGREDIENTS
8 scallops, shelled (the shells are available in cooking ware stores and some good fish markets)
2 slices fresh ginger, finely shredded
½ garlic clove, shredded
2 scallions, green parts only, shredded
salt and pepper

FOR THE SAUCE
1 garlic clove, crushed
1 tbsp fresh ginger, finely grated
2 scallions, white parts only, chopped
1–2 fresh green chilies, seeded and finely chopped
1 tbsp light soy sauce
1 tbsp dark soy sauce
2 tsp sesame oil

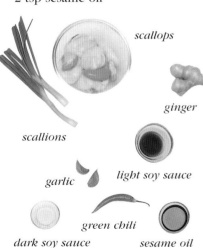

scallops

ginger

scallions

garlic

light soy sauce

dark soy sauce

green chili

sesame oil

1 Remove the dark beard-like fringe and tough muscle from the scallops.

2 Place 2 scallops in each shell. Season lightly with salt and pepper, then sprinkle the ginger, garlic and scallions on top. Place the shells in a bamboo steamer and steam for about 6 minutes, until the scallops look opaque (you may have to do this in batches).

3 Meanwhile, mix together all the sauce ingredients and pour into a small serving bowl.

4 Carefully remove each shell from the steamer, taking care not to spill the juices, and arrange them on a serving plate with the sauce bowl in the center. Serve at once.

Lemongrass-and-basil-scented Mussels

Thai flavorings of lemongrass and basil are used in this quick and easy dish.

Serves 4

INGREDIENTS
4–4½ lb fresh mussels
  in the shell
2 lemongrass stalks
handful of small fresh basil leaves
2-in piece fresh ginger
2 shallots, finely chopped
¼ pint/⅔ cup fish stock

lemongrass

mussels

fish stock

shallots

ginger

basil

1 Scrub the mussels under cold running water, scraping off any barnacles with a small sharp knife. Pull or cut off the hairy "beards". Discard any with damaged shells and any that remain open when sharply tapped.

2 Cut each lemongrass stalk in half and bruise with a rolling pin.

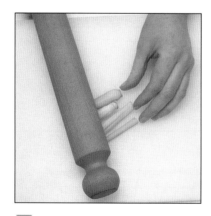

3 Coarsely chop half the basil leaves; reserve the remainder for the garnish.

4 Put the mussels, lemongrass, chopped basil, ginger, shallots and stock in a wok. Bring to a boil, cover and simmer for 5 minutes. Discard any mussels that remain closed. Sprinkle over the reserved basil and serve at once.

COOK'S TIP
Mussels are best bought fresh and eaten on the day of purchase. Any that remain closed after cooking should be thrown away.

Spiced Shrimp with Coconut

This spicy dish is based on *Sambal Goreng Udang*, which is Indonesian in origin. It is best served with plain boiled rice.

Serves 3–4

INGREDIENTS

2–3 fresh red chilies, seeded and chopped
3 shallots, chopped
1 lemongrass stalk, chopped
2 garlic cloves, chopped
thin sliver of dried shrimp paste
½ tsp ground galangal
1 tsp ground turmeric
1 tsp ground coriander
1 tbsp peanut oil
1 cup water
2 fresh kaffir lime leaves
1 tsp light brown sugar
2 tomatoes, peeled, seeded and chopped
1 cup coconut milk
1½ lb large raw shrimp, peeled and deveined
squeeze of lemon juice
salt, to taste
shredded scallions and flaked coconut, to garnish

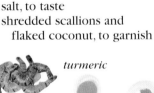
turmeric

shrimp

red chilies

coriander

garlic

lemongrass

dried shrimp paste

peanut oil

galangal

coconut milk   *sugar*

kaffir lime leaves   *tomatoes*   *shallots*

1 In a mortar pound the chilies, shallots, lemongrass, garlic, shrimp paste, galangal, turmeric and coriander with a pestle until it forms a paste.

COOK'S TIP
Dried shrimp paste, much used in Southeast Asia, is available at Asian stores.

2 Heat a wok until hot, add the oil and swirl it around. Add the spiced paste and stir-fry for about 2 minutes. Pour in the water and add the kaffir lime leaves, sugar and tomatoes. Simmer for 8–10 minutes, until most of the liquid has evaporated.

3 Add the coconut milk and shrimp and cook gently, stirring, for about 4 minutes until the shrimp are pink. Taste and adjust the seasoning with salt and a squeeze of lemon juice. Serve at once, garnished with shredded scallions and toasted flaked coconut.

Beef Rendang

In this curry from Indonesia, the meat is simmered in a mixture of coconut milk and spices until the liquid has almost disappeared, leaving dark, intensely flavored meat.

Serves 4

INGREDIENTS
4 dried red chilies
3-in piece galangal
6 shallots, chopped
1 small red bell pepper, seeded
   and chopped
4 garlic cloves, chopped
2 tsp ground cinnamon
2 tsp ground coriander
1 tsp ground turmeric
1 tsp ground cloves
1 tbsp peanut oil
6¼ cups coconut milk
2 bay leaves
2 lemongrass stalks,
   bruised
3 fresh kaffir lime leaves
2¼ lb round or flank steak,
   trimmed and cut into
   2-in cubes
1 tsp salt
shredded kaffir lime leaves and
   red chili flowers, to garnish
plain boiled rice, to serve

coriander · cloves · cinnamon · turmeric · coconut milk · steak · shallots · red pepper · garlic · galangal · red chilies · bay leaves · kaffir lime leaves · lemongrass

COOK'S TIP
This curry tastes even better if made the day before and kept covered in the fridge. Reheat it on top of the stove until piping hot before serving.

1 Crumble or break the chilies into a bowl. Add 4 tbsp water and allow to soak for 30 minutes.

2 Peel and thickly chop the galangal.

3 Put the soaked chilies and their liquid, the galangal, the chopped shallots, pepper, garlic and remaining spices into a blender or food processor and blend until smooth.

4 Heat a wok until hot, add the oil and swirl it around. Add the spice paste and stir-fry for about 2 minutes. Pour in the coconut milk and add the bay leaves, lemongrass and kaffir lime leaves. Bring to a boil, stirring constantly.

5 Add the meat and salt. Reduce the heat and simmer, uncovered for 2–2½ hours, stirring occasionally, until most of the liquid has evaporated. Towards the end of cooking, stir the meat more frequently to prevent it sticking. Taste and season if necessary. Garnish with shredded kaffir lime leaves and red chili flowers. Serve with plain boiled rice.

Paper-thin Lamb with Scallions

Scallions lend a delicious flavor to the lamb in this simple supper dish.

Serves 3–4

INGREDIENTS
1 lb lamb cutlet
2 tbsp Chinese rice wine
2 tsp light soy sauce
½ tsp roasted and ground
    Szechuan peppercorns
½ tsp salt
½ tsp dark brown sugar
4 tsp dark soy sauce
1 tbsp sesame oil
2 tbsp peanut oil
2 garlic cloves, thinly sliced
2 bunches scallions, cut
    into 3-in lengths,
    then shredded
30 ml/2 tbsp chopped
    fresh cilantro

scallions

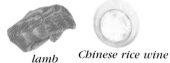
lamb   *Chinese rice wine*

sesame oil
              light soy sauce

dark soy sauce
              cilantro

brown sugar   *garlic*

1 Wrap the lamb and place in the freezer for about 1 hour, until just frozen. Cut the meat across the grain into paper-thin slices. Put the lamb slices in a bowl, add 2 tsp of the rice wine, the light soy sauce and ground Szechuan peppercorns. Mix well and allow to marinate for 15–30 minutes.

2 Make the sauce: in a bowl mix together the remaining rice wine, the salt, brown sugar, dark soy sauce and 2 tsp of the sesame oil. Set aside.

3 Heat a wok until hot, add the oil and swirl it around. Add the garlic and let it sizzle for a few seconds, then add the lamb. Stir-fry for about 1 minute, until the lamb is no longer pink. Pour in the sauce and stir briefly.

4 Add the scallions and cilantro and stir-fry for 15–20 seconds until the scallions just wilt. The finished dish should be slightly dry in appearance. Serve at once, sprinkled with the remaining sesame oil.

Chili Beef with Basil

This is a dish for chili lovers! It is very easy to prepare and cook.

Serves 2

INGREDIENTS
about 6 tbsp peanut oil
16–20 large fresh basil leaves
10 oz round steak
2 tbsp Thai fish sauce
  (*nam pla*)
1 tsp dark brown sugar
1–2 fresh red chilies, sliced
  into rings
3 garlic cloves, chopped
1 tsp finely chopped
  fresh ginger
1 shallot, thinly sliced
2 tbsp finely chopped fresh
  basil leaves
squeeze of lemon juice
salt and ground black pepper
Thai jasmine rice, to serve

steak

shallot

Thai fish sauce

basil

garlic

sugar

ginger

peanut oil

red chili

1 Heat the oil in a wok and, when hot, add the basil leaves and fry for about 1 minute, until crisp and golden. Drain on paper towels. Remove the wok from the heat and pour off all but 2 tbsp of the oil.

2 Cut the steak across the grain into thin strips. In a bowl mix together the fish sauce and sugar. Add the beef, mix well, then allow to marinate for about 30 minutes.

3 Reheat the oil until hot, add the chili(es), garlic, ginger and shallot and stir-fry for 30 seconds. Add the beef and chopped basil, then stir-fry for about 3 minutes. Flavor with lemon juice and add seasoning to taste.

4 Transfer to a serving plate, sprinkle over the basil leaves and serve immediately with Thai jasmine rice.

Lemongrass Pork

Chilies and lemongrass flavor this simple stir-fry, while peanuts add crunch.

Serves 4

INGREDIENTS

1½ lb boneless pork loin
2 lemongrass stalks,
  finely chopped
4 scallions, thinly sliced
1 tsp salt
12 black peppercorns,
  coarsely crushed
2 tbsp peanut oil
2 garlic cloves, chopped
2 fresh red chilies, seeded
  and chopped
1 tsp light brown sugar
2 tbsp Thai fish sauce (*nam pla*),
  or to taste
¼ cup roasted unsalted peanuts,
  chopped
salt and ground black pepper
rice noodles, to serve
coarsely torn cilantro leaves,
  to garnish

scallions

red chilies

peanuts

pork

sugar

cilantro

lemongrass

garlic

Thai fish sauce

peanut oil

1 Trim any excess fat from the pork. Cut the meat across into ¼-in thick slices, then cut each slice into ¼-in strips. Put the pork into a bowl with the lemongrass, scallions, salt and crushed peppercorns; mix well. Cover and allow to marinate for 30 minutes.

2 Heat a wok until hot, add the oil and swirl it around. Add the pork mixture and stir-fry for 3 minutes.

3 Add the garlic and chilies and stir-fry for another 5–8 minutes over medium heat until the pork no longer looks pink.

4 Add the sugar, fish sauce and peanuts, and toss to mix. Taste and adjust the seasoning, if necessary. Serve at once on a bed of rice noodles, garnished with coarsely torn cilantro leaves.

Spiced Lamb with Spinach

This recipe is based on *Sag Gosht* – meat cooked with spinach. The whole spices in this dish are not meant to be eaten.

Serves 3-4

INGREDIENTS

3 tbsp vegetable oil
1¼ lb lean boneless lamb,
    cut into 1-in cubes
1 onion, chopped
3 garlic cloves, finely chopped
½-in piece fresh ginger,
    finely chopped
6 black peppercorns
4 whole cloves
1 bay leaf
3 green cardamom pods, crushed
1 tsp ground cumin
1 tsp ground coriander
generous pinch of
    cayenne pepper
⅔ cup water
2 tomatoes, peeled, seeded
    and chopped
1 tsp salt
400 g/14 oz fresh spinach,
    trimmed, washed and
    finely chopped
1 tsp garam masala
crisp-fried onions and fresh
    cilantro sprigs, to garnish
nan bread or spiced basmati
    rice, to serve

1 Heat a kadhai or wok until hot. Add 2 tbsp of the oil and swirl it around. When hot, stir-fry the lamb in batches until evenly browned. Remove the lamb and set aside. Add the remaining oil, onion, garlic and ginger and stir-fry for 2–3 minutes.

2 Add the peppercorns, cloves, bay leaf, cardamom pods, cumin, coriander and cayenne pepper. Stir-fry for 30–45 seconds. Return the lamb and add the water, tomatoes and salt and bring to a boil. Simmer, covered, over very low heat for about 1 hour, stirring occasionally, until the meat is tender.

3 Increase the heat, then gradually add the spinach to the lamb, stirring to mix. Keep stirring and cooking until the spinach wilts completely and most, but not all of the liquid has evaporated and you are left with a thick green sauce. Stir in the garam masala. Garnish with crisp-fried onions and cilantro sprigs. Serve with nan bread or spiced basmati rice.

cardamom pods

onion

cloves

lamb

garlic

cayenne pepper

coriander

cumin

bay leaf

spinach

ginger

tomatoes

garam masala

Glazed Chicken with Cashew Nuts

Hoisin sauce lends a sweet yet slightly hot note to this chicken dish, while cashew nuts add a pleasing contrast of texture.

Serves 4

INGREDIENTS
¾ cup cashew nuts
1 red bell pepper
1 lb skinless and boneless
  chicken breasts
3 tbsp peanut oil
4 garlic cloves, finely chopped
2 tbsp Chinese rice wine or
  medium-dry sherry
3 tbsp hoisin sauce
2 tsp sesame oil
5–6 scallions,
  green parts only,
  cut into 1-in lengths

scallions

chicken

red pepper

cashew nuts

Chinese rice wine

garlic

peanut oil

hoisin sauce

sesame oil

1 Heat a wok until hot, add the cashew nuts and stir-fry over low to medium heat for 1–2 minutes, until golden brown. Remove and set aside.

2 Halve the pepper and remove the seeds. Slice the pepper and chicken into finger-length strips.

VARIATION
Use blanched almonds instead of cashew nuts if you prefer.

3 Heat the wok again until hot, add the oil and swirl it around. Add the garlic and let it sizzle in the oil for a few seconds. Add the pepper and chicken and stir-fry for 2 minutes.

4 Add the rice wine or sherry and hoisin sauce. Continue to stir-fry until the chicken is tender and all the ingredients are evenly glazed.

5 Stir in the sesame oil, toasted cashew nuts and scallion tips. Serve immediately with rice or noodles.

Thai Red Chicken Curry

Here chicken and potatoes are simmered in spiced coconut milk, then garnished with shredded kaffir lime leaves and red chilies.

Serves 4

INGREDIENTS
1 onion
1 tbsp peanut oil
1⅔ cups coconut milk
2 tbsp red curry paste
2 tbsp Thai fish sauce
   (*nam pla*)
1 tbsp light brown sugar
8 oz tiny new potatoes
1 lb skinless chicken breasts,
   cut into chunks
1 tbsp lime juice
2 tbsp fresh mint,
   finely chopped
1 tbsp fresh basil,
   finely chopped
2 kaffir lime leaves, shredded
1–2 fresh red chilies, seeded and
   finely shredded
salt and ground black pepper

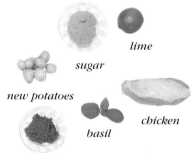

sugar   *lime*

new potatoes

basil   *chicken*

red curry paste

onion

coconut milk

mint

Thai fish sauce

VARIATION

You can use boneless chicken thighs instead of breasts. Simply skin them, cut the flesh into chunks and cook in the coconut milk with the potatoes.

1 Cut the onion into wedges.

2 Heat a wok until hot, add the oil and swirl it around. Add the onion and stir-fry for 3–4 minutes.

3 Pour in the coconut milk, then bring to a boil, stirring. Stir in the curry paste, fish sauce and sugar.

4 Add the potatoes and seasoning and simmer gently, covered, for about 20 minutes.

5 Add the chicken chunks and cook, covered, over low heat for another 5–10 minutes, until the chicken and potatoes are tender.

6 Stir in the lime juice, chopped mint and basil. Serve at once, sprinkled with the shredded kaffir lime leaves and red chilies.

Chicken Tikka Masala

This recipe is based on *Makkhani Murghi*, a popular dish. Serve with warm nan bread or fluffy basmati rice.

Serves 4

INGREDIENTS

FOR THE MARINATED CHICKEN
4 chicken breasts,
  skinned
⅔ cup plain yogurt
1-in piece fresh ginger,
  finely grated
2 garlic cloves,
  crushed
1 tsp cayenne pepper
1 tbsp ground coriander
2 tbsp vegetable oil
2 tbsp lime juice
few drops each of yellow and
  red liquid food coloring,
  mixed to a bright orange shade

FOR THE MASALA
3 oz unsalted butter
1 tbsp vegetable oil
1 onion, chopped
1 lb tomatoes, peeled,
  seeded and chopped
1 tsp salt
1 fresh green chili, seeded and
  finely chopped
1 tsp garam masala
¼ tsp cayenne pepper
½ cup heavy cream
3 tbsp plain yogurt
2 tbsp fresh cilantro leaves,
  coarsely torn
1 tsp dry-roasted cumin
  seeds

COOK'S TIP
If you can, allow the chicken to marinate for as long as possible to allow plenty of time for it to absorb the flavorings.

1 Cut each chicken breast into three or four pieces, then slash the meaty side of each piece. Put the chicken into a shallow dish. In a bowl, mix together the yogurt, ginger, garlic, chili powder, ground coriander, oil, lime juice and coloring. Pour over the chicken and toss to coat completely, making sure that the marinade goes into the slits in the chicken. Cover and leave in the fridge for 6–24 hours, turning occasionally.

2 Preheat the oven to 450°F. Lift the chicken pieces out of the marinade, shaking off any excess liquid, and then arrange in a shallow baking tin. Bake for 15–20 minutes, until golden brown and cooked through.

cayenne pepper

chicken

cilantro

tomatoes

heavy cream

cayenne pepper

ginger

butter

vegetable oil

green chili

onion

food coloring

coriander

yogurt

3 Meanwhile, make the masala: heat the butter and oil in a kadhai or wok, add the onion and fry for 5 minutes, until softened. Add the tomatoes, salt, chili, garam masala and cayenne pepper. Cook, covered, for about 10 minutes.

4 Stir in the cream and yogurt, then simmer over low heat for 1–2 minutes, stirring constantly. Add the chicken pieces, then stir to coat in the sauce. Serve at once sprinkled with cilantro leaves and roasted cumin seeds.

Stir-fried Turkey with Broccoli and Mushrooms

This is a really easy, tasty supper dish which works well with chicken too.

Serves 4

INGREDIENTS
4 oz broccoli florets
4 scallions
1 tsp cornstarch
3 tbsp oyster sauce
1 tbsp dark soy sauce
½ cup chicken stock,
  or bouillon cube
  and water
2 tsp lemon juice
3 tbsp peanut oil
1 lb turkey fillets, cut into
  strips, about ¼ x 2 in
1 small onion, chopped
2 garlic cloves, crushed
2 tsp fresh ginger,
  finely grated
4 oz fresh shiitake
  mushrooms, sliced
3 oz canned baby corn,
  halved lengthwise
1 tbsp sesame oil
salt and ground black pepper
egg noodles, to serve

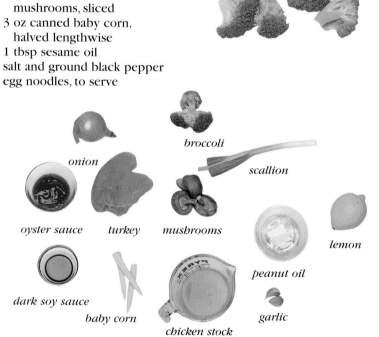

onion

broccoli

scallion

oyster sauce   turkey   mushrooms

lemon

dark soy sauce

peanut oil

baby corn   garlic

chicken stock

1 Divide the broccoli florets into smaller sprigs and cut the stalks into thin diagonal slices.

2 Finely chop the white parts of the scallions and slice the green parts into thin shreds.

3 In a bowl, blend together the cornstarch, oyster sauce, soy sauce, stock and lemon juice. Set aside.

4 Heat a wok until hot, add 2 tbsp of the peanut oil and swirl it around. Add the turkey and stir-fry for about 2 minutes, until golden and crispy at the edges. Remove the turkey from the wok and keep warm.

5 Add the remaining peanut oil to the wok and stir-fry the chopped onion, garlic and ginger over medium heat for about 1 minute. Increase the heat to high, add the broccoli, mushrooms and corn and stir-fry for 2 minutes.

6 Return the turkey to the wok, then add the sauce with the chopped scallion and seasoning. Cook, stirring, for about 1 minute, until the sauce has thickened. Then stir in the sesame oil. Serve immediately on a bed of egg noodles with the finely shredded scallion sprinkled on top.

Sweet-sour Duck with Mango

Mango adds natural sweetness to this colorful stir-fry. Crispy deep-fried noodles make the perfect accompaniment.

Serves 4

INGREDIENTS
8–12 oz duck breasts
3 tbsp dark soy sauce
1 tbsp Chinese rice wine
1 tsp sesame oil
1 tsp Chinese five-
    spice powder
1 tbsp brown sugar
2 tsp cornstarch
3 tbsp Chinese rice vinegar
1 tbsp tomato ketchup
1 mango, not too ripe
3 baby eggplant
1 red onion
1 carrot
4 tbsp peanut oil
1 garlic clove, sliced
1-in piece fresh ginger,
    cut into shreds
3 oz sugar snap peas

duck breasts · peanut oil · carrot · dark soy sauce
Chinese rice wine · mango · eggplant · sesame oil · sugar snap peas
tomato ketchup · ginger · sugar · red onion · Chinese five-spice powder · garlic

1 Thinly slice the duck breasts and place in a bowl. Mix together 1 tbsp of the soy sauce with the rice wine or sherry, sesame oil and five-spice powder. Pour over the duck, cover and allow to marinate for 1–2 hours. In a separate bowl, blend together the sugar, cornstarch, rice vinegar, ketchup and remaining soy sauce. Set aside.

2 Peel the mango, slice the flesh from the pit, then cut into thick strips. Slice the eggplant, onion and carrot into similar-sized pieces.

4 Add the remaining oil and fry the onion, garlic, ginger and carrot for 2–3 minutes, then add the sugar snap peas and stir-fry for another 2 minutes.

VARIATION

If baby eggplants are not available, use one small to medium eggplant instead.

3 Heat a wok until hot, add 2 tbsp of the oil and swirl it around. Drain the duck, reserving the marinade. Stir-fry the duck slices over high heat until the fat is crisp and golden. Remove and keep warm. Add 1 tbsp of the oil to the wok and stir-fry the eggplant for 3 minutes until golden.

5 Add the mango and return the duck with the sauce and reserved marinade to the wok. Cook, stirring, until the sauce thickens slightly. Serve at once.

VEGETABLE AND VEGETARIAN DISHES

Stir-fried Vegetables with Cilantro Omelet

This is a great supper dish for vegetarians. The glaze is added here only to make the mixture shine, it is not intended as a sauce.

Serves 3-4

INGREDIENTS
FOR THE OMELET
2 eggs
2 tbsp water
3 tbsp chopped cilantro
salt and ground black pepper
1 tbsp peanut oil

FOR THE GLAZED VEGETABLES
1 tbsp cornstarch
2 tbsp dry sherry
1 tbsp sweet chili sauce
½ cup vegetable stock, or
  vegetable bouillon cube
  and water
2 tbsp peanut oil
1 tsp fresh ginger,
  finely grated
6-8 scallions, sliced
4 oz snow peas
1 yellow bell pepper,
  seeded and sliced
4 oz fresh shiitake or
  button mushrooms
3 oz (drained weight)
  canned water chestnuts, rinsed
4 oz beansprouts
½ small Chinese cabbage,
  coarsely shredded

cilantro

egg

peanut oil

snow peas

scallion

yellow pepper

mushrooms

stock

sweet chili sauce

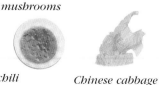
Chinese cabbage

beansprouts

1 Make the omelet: whisk the eggs, water, cilantro and seasoning in a small bowl. Heat the oil in a wok. Pour in the eggs, then tilt the wok so that the mixture spreads to an even layer. Cook over high heat until the edges are slightly crisp.

2 With a wok or spatula, flip the omelet over and cook the other side for about 30 seconds, until lightly browned. Turn the omelet onto a board and allow to cool. When cold, roll up loosely and cut into thin slices. Wipe the wok clean.

3 In a bowl, blend together the cornstarch, soy sauce, chili sauce and stock. Set aside.

4 Heat the wok until hot, add the oil and swirl it around, add the ginger and scallions and stir-fry for a few seconds to flavor the oil. Add the snow peas, pepper, mushrooms and water chestnuts and stir-fry for 3 minutes.

VARIATION
Vary the combination of vegetables used according to availability and taste.

5 Add the beansprouts and Chinese cabbage and stir-fry for 2 minutes.

6 Pour in the glaze ingredients and cook, stirring, for about 1 minute until the glaze thickens and coats the vegetables. Turn the vegetables onto a warmed serving plate and top with the omelet shreds. Serve at once.

Szechuan Eggplant

This dish is also known as fish-fragrant eggplant, as the eggplant is cooked with flavorings that are often used with fish.

Serves 4

INGREDIENTS
2 small eggplant
1 tsp salt
3 dried red chilies
peanut oil, for deep frying
3–4 garlic cloves, finely chopped
½-in piece fresh ginger,
    finely chopped
4 scallions, cut into 1-in lengths
    (white and green parts
    separated)
1 tbsp Chinese rice wine
    or medium-dry sherry
1 tbsp light soy sauce
1 tsp sugar
¼ tsp ground roasted
    Szechuan peppercorns
1 tbsp Chinese rice vinegar
1 tsp sesame oil

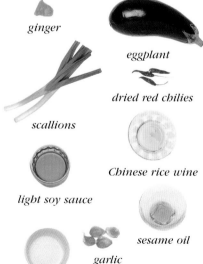

ginger

eggplant

dried red chilies

scallions

Chinese rice wine

light soy sauce

sesame oil

garlic

peanut oil

1 Trim the eggplant and cut into strips, about 1½ in wide and 3 in long. Place the eggplant in a colander and sprinkle over the salt. Set aside for 30 minutes, then rinse them thoroughly under cold running water. Pat dry with paper towels.

2 Meanwhile, soak the chilies in warm water for 15 minutes. Drain, then cut each chili into three or four pieces, discarding the seeds.

3 Half-fill a wok with oil and heat to 350°F. Deep-fry the eggplant, until golden brown. Drain on paper towels. Pour off most of the oil from the wok. Reheat the oil and add the garlic, ginger and white scallion.

4 Stir-fry for 30 seconds. Add the eggplant and toss, then add the rice wine or sherry, soy sauce, sugar, ground Szechuan peppercorns and rice vinegar. Stir-fry for 1–2 minutes. Sprinkle over the sesame oil and green scallion.

Chinese Greens with Oyster Sauce

Here Chinese greens are prepared in a very simple way – stir-fried and served with oyster sauce. The combination makes a simple, quickly prepared, tasty accompaniment.

Serves 3-4

INGREDIENTS
1 lb Chinese greens
   (*bok choy*)
2 tbsp peanut oil
1–2 tbsp oyster sauce

Chinese greens

peanut oil

oyster sauce

VARIATION

You can replace the Chinese greens with Chinese flowering cabbage, or Chinese broccoli, which is also known by its Cantonese name *choi sam*. It has green leaves and tiny yellow flowers, which are also eaten along with the leaves and stalks. It is available at Asian markets.

1 Trim the Chinese greens, removing any discolored leaves and damaged stems. Tear into manageable pieces.

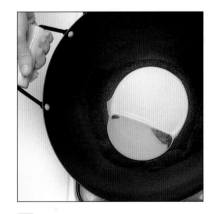

2 Heat a wok until hot, add the oil and swirl it around.

3 Add the Chinese greens and stir-fry for 2–3 minutes, until the greens have wilted a little.

4 Add the oyster sauce and continue to stir-fry a few seconds more until the greens are cooked but still slightly crisp. Serve immediately.

Deep-fried Root Vegetables with Spiced Salt

All kinds of root vegetables may be finely sliced and deep-fried to make "chips". Serve as an accompaniment to an oriental-style meal or simply by themselves as a nibble.

Serves 4–6

INGREDIENTS
1 carrot
2 parsnips
2 raw beets
1 sweet potato
peanut oil, for deep frying
¼ tsp cayenne pepper
1 tsp sea salt flakes

cayenne pepper

sweet potato

peanut oil

carrot

beet

parsnips

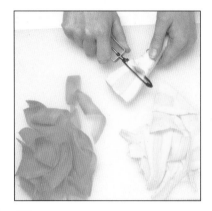

1 Peel all the vegetables, then slice the carrot and parsnips into long, thin ribbons, and the beets and sweet potato into thin rounds. Pat dry all the vegetables on paper towels.

2 Half-fill a wok with oil and heat to 350°F. Add the vegetable slices in batches and deep-fry for 2–3 minutes, until golden and crisp. Remove and drain on paper towels.

3 Place the cayenne pepper and sea salt in a mortar and grind together to a coarse powder.

4 Pile up the vegetable "chips" on a serving plate and sprinkle over the spiced salt.

COOK'S TIP
To save time, you can slice the vegetables using a mandoline or a blender or food processor with a thin slicing disc attached.

Stir-fried Spinach with Garlic and Sesame Seeds

The sesame seeds add a crunchy texture which contrasts well with the wilted spinach in this easy vegetable dish.

Serves 2

INGREDIENTS
8 oz fresh spinach, washed
1½ tbsp sesame seeds
2 tbsp peanut oil
¼ tsp sea salt flakes
2–3 garlic cloves, sliced

spinach

peanut oil

garlic

sesame seeds

1 Shake the spinach to get rid of any excess water, then remove the stalks and discard any yellow or damaged leaves. Lay several spinach leaves one on top of another, roll up tightly and cut crossways into wide strips. Repeat with the remaining leaves.

COOK'S TIP
Take care when adding the spinach to the hot oil, as it will spit furiously.

2 Heat a wok to medium heat, add the sesame seeds and dry-fry, stirring, for 1–2 minutes, until golden brown. Transfer to a small bowl and set aside.

3 Add the oil to the wok and swirl it around. When hot, add the salt, spinach and garlic and stir-fry for 2 minutes until the spinach just wilts and the leaves are coated with the oil.

4 Sprinkle over the sesame seeds and toss well. Serve at once.

Yellow Flower Vegetables

To serve, each person spreads hoisin sauce on a pancake, adds filling and rolls it up.

Serves 4

INGREDIENTS

3 eggs
2 tbsp water
4 tbsp peanut oil
1 oz dried Chinese black
　mushrooms
1 oz dried wood ears
2 tsp cornstarch
2 tbsp light soy sauce
2 tbsp Chinese rice wine or
　medium-dry sherry
2 tsp sesame oil
2 garlic cloves, finely chopped
½-in piece fresh ginger,
　cut into thin shreds
3 oz canned sliced bamboo
　shoots (drained weight), rinsed
6 oz beansprouts
4 scallions, finely shredded
salt and ground black pepper
Chinese pancakes and hoisin
　sauce, to serve

COOK'S TIP
Chinese pancakes are available at Asian markets. Reheat them in a bamboo steamer for 2-3 minutes before serving.

1 Whisk the eggs, water and seasoning in a small bowl. Heat 1 tbsp of the peanut oil in a wok and swirl it around. Pour in the eggs, then tilt the wok so that they spread to an even layer. Continue to cook over high heat for about 2 minutes, until set. Turn onto a board and, when cool, roll up and cut into thin strips. Wipe the wok clean.

2 Meanwhile, put the black mushrooms and wood ears into separate bowls. Pour over enough warm water to cover, then allow to soak for 20–30 minutes, until soft. Drain the dried mushrooms, reserving their soaking liquid. Squeeze the excess liquid from each of them.

3 Remove the tough stalks and thinly slice the black mushrooms. Finely shred the wood ears. Set aside. Strain the reserved soaking liquid through muslin into a measuring cup; reserve ½ cup of the liquid. Then, in a bowl, blend the cornstarch with the reserved liquid, soy sauce, rice wine or sherry and sesame oil.

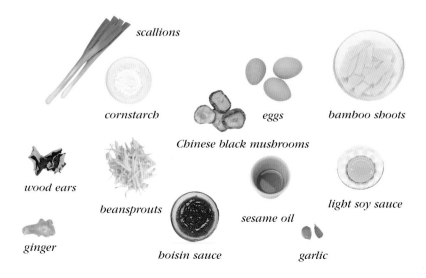

scallions

cornstarch　　　　eggs　　　bamboo shoots

Chinese black mushrooms

wood ears

beansprouts　　　　　　　　　　　　light soy sauce

　　　　　　　　sesame oil

ginger　　　hoisin sauce　　　garlic

4 Heat the wok over medium heat, add the remaining peanut oil and swirl it around. Add the wood ears and black mushrooms and stir-fry for about 2 minutes. Add the garlic, ginger, bamboo shoots and beansprouts and stir-fry for 1–2 minutes.

5 Pour in the cornstarch mixture and cook, stirring, for 1 minute until thickened. Add the scallions and omelet strips and toss gently. Adjust the seasoning, adding more soy sauce, if needed. Serve at once with the Chinese pancakes and hoisin sauce.

Spiced Coconut Mushrooms

Here is a simple and delicious way to cook mushrooms. They may be served with almost any Asian meal as well as with grilled or roasted meats and poultry.

Serves 3-4

INGREDIENTS
2 tbsp peanut oil
2 garlic cloves, finely chopped
2 fresh red chilies, seeded and sliced into rings
3 shallots, finely chopped
225 g/8 oz crimini or button mushrooms, thickly sliced
⅔ cup coconut milk
2 tbsp fresh cilantro, finely chopped
salt and ground black pepper

red chilies

coconut milk

mushrooms

peanut oil

cilantro

garlic

1 Heat a wok until hot, add the oil and swirl it around. Add the garlic and chilies, then stir-fry for a few seconds.

2 Add the shallots and stir-fry for 2–3 minutes, until softened. Add the mushrooms and stir-fry for 3 minutes.

3 Pour in the coconut milk and bring to a boil. Boil rapidly over high heat until the liquid is reduced by half and coats the mushrooms. Taste and adjust the seasoning, if necessary.

4 Sprinkle over the cilantro and toss gently to mix. Serve at once.

VARIATION
Use chopped fresh chives instead of cilantro if you wish.

Spicy Potatoes and Cauliflower

This dish is simplicity itself to make and may be eaten as a vegetarian main meal for two with Indian breads or rice, a raita, such as cucumber and yogurt, and a fresh mint relish.

Serves 2

INGREDIENTS
8 oz potatoes
5 tbsp peanut oil
1 tsp ground cumin
1 tsp ground coriander
¼ tsp ground turmeric
¼ tsp cayenne pepper
1 fresh green chili, seeded and
   finely chopped
1 medium cauliflower, broken up
   into small florets
1 tsp cumin seeds
2 garlic cloves, cut into shreds
1–2 tbsp fresh coriander
   finely chopped
salt, to taste

cumin seeds   *potatoes*

coriander   *cilantro*   *cayenne pepper*   *turmeric*

cumin   *cauliflower*   *garlic*
green chili

1   Boil the potatoes in their skins in boiling, salted water for about 20 minutes, until just tender. Drain and let cool. When cool enough to handle, peel and cut into 1-in cubes.

2   Heat 3 tbsp of the oil in a kadhai or wok. When hot, add the ground cumin, coriander, turmeric, cayenne pepper and chili. Let the spices sizzle for a few seconds.

3   Add the cauliflower and about 4 tbsp water. Cook, stirring continuously, for 6–8 minutes over medium heat. Add the potatoes and stir-fry for 2–3 minutes. Season to taste, then remove from the heat.

4   Heat the remaining oil in a small frying pan. When hot, add the cumin seeds and garlic and cook until lightly browned. Pour the mixture over the vegetables. Sprinkle with the chopped cilantro and serve at once.

Red-cooked Tofu with Chinese Mushrooms

Red-cooked is a term applied to Chinese dishes cooked with dark soy sauce. This tasty dish can be served as either a side dish or main meal.

Serves 2-4

INGREDIENTS
8 oz firm tofu
3 tbsp dark soy sauce
2 tbsp Chinese rice wine or
    medium-dry sherry
2 tsp dark brown sugar
1 garlic clove, crushed
1 tbsp fresh ginger,
    finely grated
2.5 ml/½ tsp Chinese five-
    spice powder
pinch of ground roasted
    Szechuan peppercorns
6 dried Chinese black mushrooms
1 tsp cornstarch
2 tbsp peanut oil
5-6 scallions, sliced into
    1-in lengths
rice noodles, to serve
small basil leaves, to garnish

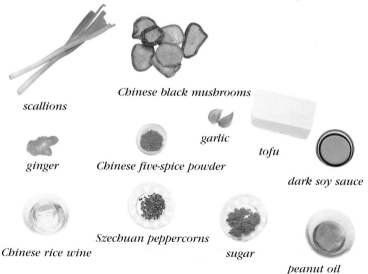

scallions

Chinese black mushrooms

garlic

tofu

ginger

Chinese five-spice powder

dark soy sauce

Chinese rice wine

Szechuan peppercorns

sugar

peanut oil

1 Drain the tofu, pat dry with paper towels and cut into 1-in cubes. Place in a shallow dish. In a small bowl, mix together the soy sauce, rice wine or sherry, sugar, garlic, ginger, five-spice powder and Szechuan peppercorns. Pour the marinade over the tofu, toss well and let marinate for about 30 minutes. Drain, reserving the marinade.

2 Meanwhile, soak the dried black mushrooms in warm water for 20–30 minutes until soft. Drain, reserving 6 tbsp of the soaking liquid. Squeeze out any excess liquid from the mushrooms, remove the tough stalks and slice the caps. In a small bowl, blend the cornstarch with the reserved marinade and mushroom soaking liquid.

3 Heat a wok until hot, add the oil and swirl it around. Add the tofu and fry for 2–3 minutes, until evenly golden. Remove from the wok and set aside.

4 Add the mushrooms and white scallions to the wok and stir-fry for 2 minutes. Pour in the marinade mixture and stir for 1 minute, until thickened.

5 Return the tofu to the wok with the green scallions. Simmer gently for 1–2 minutes. Serve at once with rice noodles and sprinkled with basil leaves.

Spicy ChickPeas with Fresh Ginger

Chickpeas are filling, nourishing and cheap. Here they are served with a refreshing raita made with scallions and mint. Serve as a snack or as part of a main meal.

Serves 4-6

INGREDIENTS
8 oz dried chickpeas
2 tbsp vegetable oil
1 small onion, chopped
1½-in piece fresh ginger, finely chopped
2 garlic cloves, finely chopped
¼ tsp ground turmeric
1 lb tomatoes, peeled, seeded and chopped
2 tbsp cilantro, finely chopped
2 tsp garam masala
salt and pepper
fresh cilantro sprigs, to garnish

FOR THE RAITA
⅔ cup plain yogurt
2 scallions, finely chopped
1 tsp roasted cumin seeds
2 tbsp chopped fresh mint
pinch of cayenne pepper, or to taste

scallions

garam masala

tomatoes

cilantro

onion

garlic

ginger

mint

plain yogurt

chickpeas

turmeric

cumin seeds

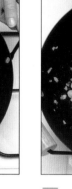

1 Put the chickpeas in a large bowl and pour over enough cold water to cover. Allow to soak overnight. The next day, drain the chickpeas and put them in a large pan with fresh cold water to cover. Bring to a boil, then boil hard for 10 minutes. Lower the heat and simmer gently for 1½–2 hours, until tender. Drain well.

2 Heat a kadhai or wok until hot, add the oil and swirl it around. Add the onion and stir-fry for 2–3 minutes, then add the ginger, garlic and turmeric. Stir-fry for a few seconds more.

3 Add the tomatoes, chickpeas and seasoning, bring to a boil, then simmer for 10–15, until the tomatoes have reduced to a thick sauce.

4 Meanwhile, make the raita: mix together the yogurt, scallions, roasted cumin seeds, mint and cayenne pepper to taste. Set aside.

VARIATION
You can replace the dried chickpeas with 2 x 15-oz cans chickpeas. Drain and rinse thoroughly before adding to the tomatoes in step 3.

5 Just before the end of cooking, stir the chopped cilantro and garam masala into the chickpeas. Serve at once, garnished with cilantro sprigs and accompanied by the raita.

RICE AND NOODLES

Crispy Noodles with Mixed Vegetables

In this dish, rice vermicelli noodles are deep-fried until crisp, then tossed into a colorful selection of stir-fried vegetables.

Serves 3-4

INGREDIENTS
2 large carrots
2 zucchini
4 scallions
4 oz Chinese long beans or
   green beans
4 oz dried vermicelli rice noodles
   or cellophane noodles
peanut oil, for deep frying
1-in piece fresh ginger,
   cut into shreds
1 fresh red chili, sliced
4 oz fresh shiitake or
   button mushrooms,
   thickly sliced
few Chinese cabbage leaves,
   coarsely shredded
3 oz beansprouts
2 tbsp light soy sauce
2 tbsp Chinese rice wine
1 tsp sugar
2 tbsp cilantro leaves,
   coarsely torn

scallions

mushrooms

Chinese long beans

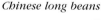
cilantro

beansprouts

red chilies

carrot

Chinese cabbage

zucchini

ginger

Chinese rice wine

light soy sauce

COOK'S TIP
If a milder flavor is preferred, remove the seeds from the chili.

1 Cut the carrots and zucchini into fine sticks, and then shred the scallions into similar-size pieces. Trim the beans. If using Chinese long beans, cut them into short lengths.

2 Break the noodles into lengths of about 3 in. Half-fill a wok with oil and heat it to 350°F. Deep-fry the raw noodles, about a handful at a time, for 1–2 minutes, until puffed and crispy. Drain on paper towels. Carefully pour off all but 2 tbsp of the oil.

3 Reheat the oil in the wok. When hot, add the beans and stir-fry for 2–3 minutes. Add the ginger, red chili, mushrooms, carrots and zucchini and stir-fry for 1–2 minutes.

4 Add the Chinese cabbage, beansprouts and scallions Stir-fry for 1 minute, then add the soy sauce, rice wine and sugar. Cook, stirring, for about 30 seconds.

5 Add the noodles and cilantro and toss to mix, taking care not to crush the noodles too much. Serve at once, piled up on a plate.

Stir-fried Tofu and Beansprouts with Noodles

This is a satisfying dish, which is both tasty and easy to make.

Serves 4

INGREDIENTS
8 oz firm tofu
peanut oil, for deep frying
6 oz medium egg noodles
1 tbsp sesame oil
1 tsp cornstarch
2 tsp dark soy sauce
1 tbsp Chinese rice wine
1 tsp sugar
6–8 scallions, cut diagonally into
    1-in lengths
3 garlic cloves, sliced
1 fresh green chili, seeded
    and sliced
4 oz Chinese cabbage leaves,
    coarsely shredded
2 oz beansprouts
2 oz cashew nuts, toasted

scallions

garlic

sesame oil

Chinese cabbage

tofu

noodles

beansprouts

dark soy sauce

Chinese rice wine

green chili

1 Drain the tofu and pat dry with paper towels. Cut the tofu into 1-in cubes. Half-fill a wok with peanut oil and heat to 350°F. Deep-fry the tofu in batches for 1–2 minutes, until golden and crisp. Drain on paper towels. Carefully pour all but 2 tbsp of the oil from the wok.

2 Cook the noodles. Rinse them thoroughly under cold water and drain well. Toss in 2 tsp of the sesame oil and set aside. In a bowl, blend together the cornstarch, soy sauce, rice wine, sugar and remaining sesame oil.

3 Reheat the 2 tbsp of peanut oil and, when hot enough, add the lengths of scallion, sliced garlic, sliced chili, shredded Chinese cabbage and beansprouts. Stir-fry for 1–2 minutes.

4 Add the tofu with the noodles and sauce. Cook, stirring, for about 1 minute, until well mixed. Sprinkle over the cashew nuts. Serve at once.

Cellophane Noodles with Pork

Unlike other types of noodle, cellophane noodles can be successfully reheated.

Serves 3-4

INGREDIENTS
4 oz cellophane noodles
4 dried Chinese black
    mushrooms
8 oz boneless lean pork
2 tbsp dark soy sauce
2 tbsp Chinese rice wine
2 garlic cloves, crushed
1 tbsp fresh ginger
    finely grated
1 tsp chili oil
3 tbsp peanut oil
4-6 scallions, chopped
1 tsp cornstarch blended with
    ¾ cup chicken stock or water
2 tbsp cilantro,
    finely chopped
salt and ground black pepper
cilantro sprigs, to garnish

scallions

noodles

chicken stock   *Chinese rice wine*

mushrooms

dark soy sauce

pork

chili oil   *peanut oil*

1 Put the noodles and mushrooms in separate bowls and pour over warm water to cover. Let soak for 15–20 minutes until soft; drain well. Cut the noodles into 5 in lengths, using scissors or a knife. Squeeze out any water from the mushrooms, discard the stems and then finely chop the caps.

2 Meanwhile, cut the pork into very small cubes. Put into a bowl with the soy sauce, rice wine, garlic, ginger and chili oil, then let stand for about 15 minutes. Drain, reserving the marinade.

3 Heat a wok until hot, add the oil and swirl it around. Add the pork and mushrooms and stir-fry for 3 minutes. Add the scallions and stir-fry for 1 minute. Stir in the cornstarch, marinade and seasoning. Cook for about 1 minute.

4 Add the noodles and stir-fry for about 2 minutes, until the noodles absorb most of the liquid and the pork is cooked through. Stir in the chopped cilantro. Taste and adjust the seasoning. Serve garnished with cilantro sprigs.

Spicy Fried Rice Sticks with Shrimp

This recipe is based on the classic Thai noodle dish called *Pad Thai*. Popular all over Thailand, it is enjoyed morning, noon and night.

VARIATION

For a vegetarian dish omit the dried shrimp and replace the jumbo shrimp with cubes of deep-fried tofu.

Serves 4

INGREDIENTS
½ oz dried shrimp
1 tbsp tamarind pulp
3 tbsp Thai fish sauce
  (*nam pla*)
1 tbsp sugar
2 garlic cloves, chopped
2 fresh red chilies, seeded and
  chopped
3 tbsp peanut oil
2 eggs, beaten
8 oz dried rice sticks, soaked in
  warm water for 30 minutes,
  refreshed under cold running
  water and drained
8 oz cooked peeled
  jumbo shrimp
3 scallions, cut into
  1-in lengths
3 oz beansprouts
2 tbsp coarsely chopped
  roasted unsalted peanuts
2 tbsp fresh cilantro,
  finely chopped
lime slices, to garnish

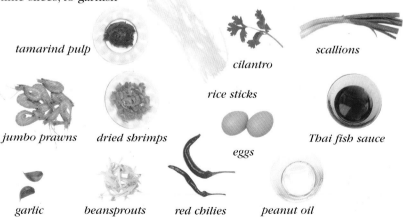

tamarind pulp   *cilantro*   *scallions*   *rice sticks*   *jumbo prawns*   *dried shrimps*   *eggs*   *Thai fish sauce*   *garlic*   *beansprouts*   *red chilies*   *peanut oil*

1 Put the dried shrimp in a small bowl and pour over enough warm water to cover. Let soak for 30 minutes until soft, then drain.

2 Put the tamarind pulp in a bowl and add 4 tbsp hot water. Blend together, then press through a sieve to extract 2 tbsp thick tamarind water. Mix the tamarind water with the fish sauce and sugar.

3 Using a mortar and pestle, pound the garlic and chilies to form a paste. Heat a wok over medium heat, add 1 tbsp of the oil, then add the beaten eggs and stir for 1–2 minutes, until the eggs are scrambled. Remove and set aside. Wipe the wok clean.

4 Reheat the wok until hot, add the remaining oil, then the chili paste and dried shrimp and stir-fry for 1 minute. Add the rice sticks and tamarind mixture and stir-fry for 3–4 minutes.

5 Add the scrambled eggs, shrimp, scallions, beansprouts, peanuts and cilantro, then stir-fry for 2 minutes, until well mixed. Serve at once, garnishing each portion with lime slices.

Indonesian Fried Rice

This fried rice dish makes an ideal supper on its own or as an accompaniment.

Serves 4-6

INGREDIENTS
4 shallots, coarsely chopped
1 fresh red chili, seeded
    and chopped
1 garlic clove, chopped
thin sliver of dried shrimp paste
3 tbsp vegetable oil
8 oz boneless lean pork, cut into
    fine strips
1¼ cups long-grain white rice,
    boiled and cooled
3-4 scallions, thinly sliced
4 oz cooked peeled shrimp
2 tbsp sweet soy sauce
    (*kecap manis*)
chopped fresh cilantro and
    fine cucumber shreds,
    to garnish

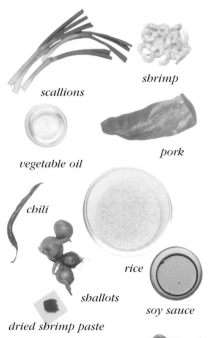

scallions

shrimp

vegetable oil

pork

chili

rice

shallots

soy sauce

dried shrimp paste

garlic

1 In a mortar pound the shallots, chili, garlic and shrimp paste with a pestle until they form a paste.

2 Heat a wok until hot, then add 2 tbsp of the oil and swirl it around. Add the pork and stir-fry for 2–3 minutes. Remove the pork from the wok, set aside and keep warm.

3 Add the remaining oil to the wok. When hot, add the spiced shallot paste and stir-fry for about 30 seconds.

4 Reduce the heat. Add the rice, scallions and shrimp. Stir-fry for 2–3 minutes. Add the pork and sprinkle over the soy sauce. Stir-fry for 1 minute. Serve garnished with the chopped cilantro and cucumber shreds.

Fried Rice with Spices

This dish is mildly spiced, suitable as an accompaniment to any curried dish. The whole spices are not meant to be eaten.

Serves 3-4

INGREDIENTS
1¼ cups basmati rice
½ tsp salt
1 tbsp ghee or butter
8 whole cloves
4 green cardamom pods, bruised
1 bay leaf
3 in cinnamon stick
1 tsp black peppercorns
1 tsp cumin seeds
1 tsp coriander seeds

rice

ghee   *coriander*

bay leaf

cinnamon stick

cardamom   *cumin*

cloves

1 Put the rice in a colander and wash thoroughly under cold running water until the water clears. Put in a bowl and pour 2½ cups fresh water over the rice. Allow the rice to soak for 30 minutes; then drain thoroughly.

2 Put the rice, salt and 2½ cups water in a heavy-bottomed pan. Bring to a boil, then simmer, covered, for about 10 minutes. The rice should be just cooked with still a little bite to it. Drain off any excess water, fluff up the grains with a fork, then spread it out on a tray and let cool.

3 Heat the ghee or butter in a kadhai or wok until foaming, add the spices and stir-fry for 1 minute.

4 Add the cooled rice and stir-fry for 3–4 minutes, until warmed through. Serve at once.

VARIATION
You could add ½ tsp ground turmeric to the rice in step 2 to color it yellow.

Thai Fried Rice

This hot and spicy dish is easy to prepare and makes a meal in itself.

VARIATION
Add 2 oz frozen peas to the chicken in step 3, if you wish.

Serves 4

INGREDIENTS
8 oz Thai jasmine rice
3 tbsp vegetable oil
1 onion, chopped
1 small red bell pepper, seeded
    and cut into ¾-in cubes
12 oz skinless and boneless
    chicken breasts, cut into
    ¾-in cubes
1 garlic clove, crushed
1 tbsp mild curry paste
½ tsp paprika
½ tsp ground turmeric
2 tbsp Thai fish sauce
    (*nam pla*)
2 eggs, beaten
salt and ground black pepper
fried basil leaves, to garnish

rice

Thai fish sauce

chicken

curry paste

onion

egg

red pepper

paprika

turmeric

vegetable oil

1 Put the rice in a sieve and wash thoroughly under cold running water. Then put the rice in a heavy-bottomed pan and add 6¼ cups boiling water. Return to a boil, then simmer, leaving the pan uncovered, for 8–10 minutes; drain well. Spread out the grains on a tray and set aside to cool.

2 Heat a wok until hot, add 2 tbsp of the oil and swirl it around. Add the onion and red pepper and stir-fry for 1 minute.

3 Add the chicken, garlic, curry paste and spices and stir-fry for 2–3 minutes.

4 Reduce the heat to medium, add the cooled rice, fish sauce and seasoning. Stir-fry for 2–3 minutes, until the rice is very hot.

5 Make a well in the center of the rice and add the remaining oil. When hot, add the beaten eggs, allow to cook for about 2 minutes until lightly set, then stir into the rice.

6 Sprinkle over the fried basil leaves and serve at once.

Stir-fried Noodles with Sweet Soy Salmon

Teriyaki sauce forms the marinade for the salmon in this recipe. Served with soft-fried noodles, it makes a stunning dish.

Serves 4

INGREDIENTS
12 oz salmon fillet
2 tbsp Japanese soy
  sauce (*shoyu*)
2 tbsp sake
4 tbsp mirin or
  sweet sherry
1 tsp light brown sugar
2 tsp fresh ginger
  finely grated
3 garlic cloves, 1 crushed, and
  2 sliced into rounds
2 tbsp peanut oil
8 oz dried egg noodles,
  cooked and drained
2 oz alfalfa sprouts
2 tbsp sesame seeds,
  lightly toasted

garlic
sesame seeds
noodles
alfalfa sprouts
sake
mirin
salmon
sugar
Japanese soy sauce
peanut oil
ginger

COOK'S TIP
It is important to scrape the marinade off the fish as any remaining pieces of ginger or garlic would burn during broiling and spoil the finished dish.

1 Thinly slice the salmon, then place in a shallow dish.

2 In a bowl, mix together the soy sauce, sake, mirin or sherry, sugar, ginger and crushed garlic. Pour over the salmon, cover and leave for 30 minutes.

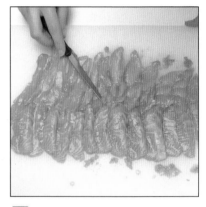

3 Preheat the broiler. Drain the salmon, scraping off and reserving the marinade. Place the salmon in a single layer on a baking sheet. Cook under the broiler for 2–3 minutes without turning.

4 Meanwhile, heat a wok until hot, add the oil and swirl it around. Add the garlic rounds and cook until golden brown but not burnt.

5 Add the cooked noodles and reserved marinade to the wok and stir-fry for 3–4 minutes, until the marinade has reduced slightly to a syrupy glaze and coats the noodles.

6 Toss in the alfalfa sprouts, then remove immediately from the heat. Transfer to warmed serving plates and top with the salmon. Sprinkle over the toasted sesame seeds. Serve at once.

Singapore Noodles

A delicious supper dish with a stunning mix of flavors and textures.

Serves 4

INGREDIENTS

8 oz dried egg noodles
3 tbsp peanut oil
1 onion, chopped
1-in piece fresh ginger,
    finely chopped
1 garlic clove,
    finely chopped
1 tbsp Madras curry powder
½ tsp salt
4 oz cooked chicken or pork,
    finely shredded
4 oz cooked peeled shrimp
4 oz Chinese cabbage leaves,
    shredded
4 oz beansprouts
4 tbsp chicken stock
1–2 tbsp dark soy sauce
1–2 fresh red chilies, seeded
    and finely shredded
4 scallions, finely shredded

beansprouts

noodles

Chinese cabbage

ginger

curry powder

chicken

dark soy sauce

onion

stock

scallions

red chilies

peanut oil

shrimp

1 Cook the noodles according to the package instructions. Rinse thoroughly under cold water and drain well. Toss in 1 tbsp of the oil and set aside.

2 Heat a wok until hot, add the remaining oil and swirl it around. Add the onion, ginger and garlic and stir-fry for about 2 minutes.

3 Add the curry powder and salt, stir-fry for 30 seconds, then add the egg noodles, chicken or pork and shrimp. Stir-fry for 3–4 minutes.

4 Add the Chinese cabbage and beansprouts and stir-fry for 1–2 minutes. Sprinkle in the stock and soy sauce to taste and toss well until evenly mixed. Serve at once, garnished with the shredded red chilies and scallions.

Noodles with Ginger and Cilantro

Here is a simple noodle dish that goes well with most Asian dishes. It can also be served as a snack for 2-3 people.

Serves 4-6

INGREDIENTS
handful of fresh cilantro sprigs
8 oz dried egg noodles
3 tbsp peanut oil
2-in piece fresh root ginger, cut
   into fine shreds
6-8 scallions, cut into shreds
2 tbsp light soy sauce
salt and ground black pepper

scallions

peanut oil

ginger

cilantro   *noodles*

light soy sauce

COOK'S TIP
Italian noodles are often the easiest to buy. They range in size from very thin to broad. Allow 2 oz per person as a side dish, and up to 4 oz for a main dish.

1 Strip the leaves from the cilantro stalks. Pile them on a chopping board and coarsely chop them, using a cleaver or large sharp knife.

2 Cook the noodles according to the instructions on the package. Rinse under cold water and drain well. Toss in 1 tbsp of the oil.

3 Heat a wok until hot, add the remaining oil and swirl it around. Add the ginger and stir-fry for a few seconds, then add the noodles and scallions. Stir-fry for 3–4 minutes, until hot.

4 Sprinkle over the soy sauce, cilantro and seasoning. Toss well, then serve at once.